MAKIN
OF RELIGIOUS
PLURALISM

Shaping theology of religions
for our times

ALAN RACE

First published in Great Britain in 2013

Society for Promoting Christian Knowledge
36 Causton Street
London SW1P 4ST
www.spckpublishing.co.uk

The author and publisher have made every effort to ensure that the external website and email
addresses included in this book are correct and up to date at the time of going to press.
The author and publisher are not responsible for the content, quality or
continuing accessibility of the sites.

Unless otherwise noted, Scripture quotations are taken from the New Revised Standard
Version of the Bible, Anglicized Edition, copyright © 1989, 1995 by the Division of
Christian Education of the National Council of the Churches of Christ in the USA.
Used by permission. All rights reserved.

British Library Cataloguing-in-Publication Data
A catalogue record for this book is available from the British Library

ISBN 978–0–281–06438–0
eBook ISBN 978–0–281–07105–0

Typeset by Graphicraft Limited, Hong Kong
First printed in Great Britain by Ashford Colour Press
Subsequently digitally printed in Great Britain

eBook by Graphicraft Limited, Hong Kong

Produced on paper from sustainable forests

Contents

About the author

Alan Race is Rector of St Margaret's Church, Lee, in south London. He has written and edited numerous books and articles in the fields of the Christian theology of religions and interfaith dialogue. These include the classic *Christians and Religious Pluralism* (SCM Press, 1983; 2nd edn, 1993) which helped to shape discussion of the subject area for many years, and *Interfaith Encounter* (SCM Press, 2001). He has been involved in parish ministry, Christian education work and international collaboration for global interfaith dialogue throughout his ordained ministry. He is editor-in-chief of the international journal, *Interreligious Insight*.

*This book is dedicated to my friends
in Christian movements working for
progressive change and
a new understanding of Christian thought
in relation to the world religions*

Acknowledgements

I would like to thank those who have contributed to this book in many untold ways. In particular I am grateful to the Revd Sonya Brown for reading the original drafts and offering many thoughtful comments for improvement.

Introduction

'In this aeon diversity of religions is the will of God.'[1]

These words from the great Jewish sage, Abraham Joshua Heschel (1907–72), indicate that for him no religion has a monopoly on holiness or spiritual insight. Heschel's point about the religions is that they are 'a means, not the end'.[2] Moreover, the notion that religious diversity is God's will is not so much a function of humanity's cultural differences as of the transcendence of God, for 'No word is God's last word, no word is God's ultimate word.'[3] Why, therefore, should our human openness to God issue only in one community of faithfulness?

In 1966, Heschel's bold affirmation was ahead of its time – for Jews as well as Christians. Christian theologians are catching up with the boldness and many are beginning to agree with Heschel, but it has taken theological thought half a century to embrace this realization.

Heschel is an example of one religious scholar's response to the globalization of religion – by which I mean the increased awareness about and access to the religions, whether that awareness and access be through human encounter or education. Since Heschel's day globalization has intensified greatly. Through modern media and the movement of peoples around the world, we are struck by the diversity of religions more than ever before. This means of course that even if you have never met a Sikh or a Jew or a Muslim or a Hindu, etc., you are likely to have an opinion about such believers and the religions they represent. But in the absence of real meeting that opinion is bound to be stereotypical at best and could well be even seriously distorted.

This is because one of the new requirements of our time is the insistence on meeting people as a way of becoming informed about what a religion stands for. It is an improvement on the older reliance on travellers' tales or second-hand accounts in books which had an axe to grind.

Affirming religious plurality as not only a human but also a divine good can be unnerving, especially for the so-called monotheistic religions such as Judaism, Christianity and Islam. But I believe the same holds true for those traditions which are often assumed to be more accepting of plurality, such as Hinduism or Buddhism. All traditions which are ordered in terms of what I call 'transcendent vision and human transformation' have a tendency to want to pull others into the ambit of their own sacred space, no matter how much they declare themselves to be universally minded. Difference might not only render human beings curious about the world around them but also generate fear and uncertainty, which in turn potentially opens the door to conflict.

Heschel's daring judgement about religious plurality is not shared by every religious thinker, then or now. Nevertheless, even those Christian theologians who might disagree with him are coming to see that at least the question of plurality is deserving of serious theological debate. This must be so, once we realize that other religions function in much the same way for their adherents as Christian faith does for Christians – that is, they all provide a matrix for responding to the mystery of existence in terms of a notion of transcendent reality and its consequent ramifications for shaping a meaningful life.

This book is about how to interpret the fact of many religions and it concentrates on what we call the 'world religions', for this has been the focus of most of the theological debate over the past fifty years or so. The term theology of religions is concerned with questions of how to interpret religious plurality as a matter of Christian understanding. Are the non-Christian world religions part of the will of God or deviations from that will, as Christian faith has often construed it?[4] The discipline is primarily concerned with religions as vehicles or mediations of transcendent truth and relationship and not with individual attitudes towards other religious people. It is necessary to point this out as there has been considerable confusion over the lack of a clear distinction between the two.

A good point of entry into the whole discussion is to feel the impact of Heschel's boldness. I call it bold because although we may have been aware of the diversity of religions – of course there have always been many religions in the world![5] – we have not thought that this called for deeper reflection than the default response that they are at best pale reflections of something altogether more profound, namely the Christian revelation. Until now, to think otherwise was tantamount to theological error and even apostasy.

Part of the methodology of theology of religions involves us in making a judgement about whether or not Christian faith can be responsive to new information. Those for whom Christian understanding has been decided and defined once and for all will measure any new information within its inherited frame of reference. In other words, Bible and Tradition (in reality, a certain view of the Bible and a certain view of Tradition) will determine the answer. Those for whom Christian understanding has always been a matter of adjustment and change according to new information – and it might be new information stemming from the natural sciences or from analyses of human behaviour in the humanities – will place equal emphasis on experience and reason in their theological work. This book is written believing theology ought to be a journey which is actively alert to new information and is constantly therefore in need of revision.

The experience, knowledge and impact of other religions represents considerable new lived information for theological reflection and the theology of religions analyses the bearing this has on Christian thought, positively and negatively. In turn, Christian thought will need to make its next adjustment for its next phase in Christian history.

The one and the many

Given the mushrooming literature on the subject of how Christian theology is responding to new lived information from other religions, inevitably a spectrum of Christian responses is emerging and this book will explore some of those responses. The responses are informed by a number of factors, including: the experience of Christian missions of the past 300 years; the rise of interreligious dialogue, which although not wholly new, nevertheless is being shaped by new parameters and assumptions; daily encounters as neighbours are having to learn new ways of living and working together; and educational materials which exceed in quality many publications of previous generations.

Before outlining some of the main contours of various positions being adopted in the Christian debate I would like to illustrate how reflection on the experience of religious plurality is often framed as a function of either quietist private piety or quarrelsome public confrontation, and I shall do this with a vivid example from literary fiction. This might help to clarify the discipline of theology of religions more closely.

In his novel, *Life of Pi*, award-winning author Yann Martel depicts his hero, Pi, as a youth who is attracted to three religions and who absorbs the central impact of these traditions into his own developing maturity. His initial religious love stems from the fact that he is born into a Hindu way of life:

I feel at home in a Hindu temple. I am aware of Presence, not
personal the way we usually feel presence, but something larger.
My heart still skips a beat when I catch sight of the murti, of God
Residing, in the inner sanctum of a temple . . . My hands naturally
come together in reverent worship. I hunger for prasad, that sugary
offering to God that comes back to us as a sanctified treat. My
palms need to feel the heat of a hallowed flame whose blessing
I bring to my eyes and forehead.[6]

Anyone who has attended Hindu worship practice will have
witnessed the blessings received by the devotee through *prasad*
and fire, each enacting a spirituality based on the unity of all
reality; as Martel has it: 'The finite within the infinite, the
infinite within the finite.'[7] For it is not only the ritual that
attracts Pi, it is also the philosophy. There are many Christians
who have drunk deeply enough at the well of the Hindu
sensibility to know the extent of its resonance with Christian
spirituality.[8]

Pi is next attracted to Christianity, or rather, to the figure of
Jesus. After encountering a Catholic priest and being troubled
by Christian notions of sacrifice and portrayals of miracles
(feeding, healing), he nevertheless feels himself attracted to
Jesus himself. Pi admits: 'I couldn't get him out of my head.
Still can't. I spent three solid days thinking about Him. The
more He bothered me, the less I could forget Him. And the
more I learned about Him, the less I wanted to leave Him.'[9]
Pi learns that the characteristic ethic of Christian faith is love.
He finally returns 'to offer thanks to Lord Krishna for having
put Jesus of Nazareth, whose humanity I found so compelling,
in my way'.[10]

Pi's third 'conversion' is to Islam, where he discovers 'a beautiful religion of brotherhood and devotion'.[11] He makes acquaintance
with Mr Kumar, a baker, Sufi practitioner and mystic, who
teaches Pi that 'If you take two steps towards God, God runs

to you.'[12] Pi learns through his contact with the baker that the whole earth is filled with the glory of God:

> One such time I left town and on my way back, at a point where the land was high and I could see the sea to my left and down the road a long ways, I suddenly felt I was in heaven. The spot was in fact no different from when I had passed it not long before, but my way of seeing it had changed. The feeling, a paradoxical mix of pulsing energy and profound peace, was intense and blissful. Whereas before the road, the sea, the trees, the air, the sun all spoke differently to me, now they spoke one language of unity . . . I knelt a mortal; I rose an immortal.[13]

This account fits the pattern of what some scholars call 'unitive mysticism', the sense that the whole of life is harmonious because our experience of it is a function of our relationship with the all-encompassing reality of the divine. While this may not be the experience of everyone who visits a mosque, nevertheless the impression of selfless devotion in the company of others and before the holy transcendence of God cannot be missed.

Pi's experience seems reminiscent of the sentiment expressed by the Islamic poet, Rumi, that 'The lamps are many, but the light is one: it comes from Beyond.'[14]

Pi is a character in a novel, but the experience of feeling attracted to a religious outlook by whatever route has presented itself is open to any human being. Something special, unavoidable and life-enhancing makes its impression and it is for us to fold that into our understanding of the world. Occasionally such experiences burst the bounds of what we have come to take for granted or to value so far. When this happens it would be small-minded, even wrong, to ignore its impact.

But the positive construal of multireligious insights creates a problem for the theologian and most often for the representative defenders of religious tradition. This is also true in

Pi's case. The three official clerical leaders are confused and outraged by Pi's multiple affiliations. The Christian Priest, the Muslim Imam and the Hindu Pandit fall to wrangling about who is the greatest in the competition between religions. Each claims Pi as his own, but in their wrangling all three demonstrate their narrow-mindedness, lack of charity and failure to comprehend how it is that the divine might be greater than any one person's or tradition's perception. Still, the Pandit speaks for all three when he says: 'But he [Pi] can't be a Hindu, a Christian *and* a Muslim. It's impossible. He must choose.'[15] That is how many a representative theologian, from whatever tradition, sees the matter.

It is possible to frame the issue of religious plurality in terms of 'new experiences' versus 'established tradition'. Through new friendships, the impressions of authentic lives lived within different matrices of belief and practice, the 'transcendent vision and human transformation' being effected in strange yet resonant forms – all this provides new lived information which religious tradition is called upon to interpret. The absorption of more than one expression of piety by a single human being may harbour elements of naivety, but the Pi fiction makes clear that it is not really possible to ignore the reality of what comes through experience. According to Pi, Heschel's speculative prospect for the future – 'In this aeon diversity of religions is the will of God' – is confirmed with a resounding 'Yes'.

On the other hand, the religions are so very different. The Priest, Pandit and Imam are presumably entitled to defend their corners, though in the novel they do so while simultaneously exhibiting remarkable ignorance of one another, but – more than this – none is prepared to hear the others as each himself wants to trumpet his own tradition. The Priest, Imam and Pandit break the first rule of interreligious dialogue, which is not to compare the best of one's own religious heritage with the worst of others. It is a short step from religious ignorance to bigotry, antagonism and even violence – as history shows.

The common default position that the religions are 'all the same really' (possibly Pi's position), and the equally strongly held position that they are destined to mutual incomprehension/ antagonism (definitely the 'official' position), I believe represent two extremes. But they are not the only responses to be found. As a kind of *via media*, the task of theology of religions is to reflect on the relationship between the unity of reality, which all traditions affirm in their different ways, and the facts of phenomenological difference between religious views of that reality. And to that we now turn.

1
Using Scripture in theology of religions

The application of Scripture in the context of coming to a Christian understanding of the place of other religions in the purposes of God is bound to be indirect. Why do I say this? There is one good reason, for a start: the Bible knows nothing of the major world religions which we can read about in any religious studies textbook, such Buddhism, Hinduism, Jainism, Islam, Sikhism, Baha'i, Taoism, Daoism, indigenous religions from the Pacific, African or American regions of the world, and so on. This would seem to be a serious defect when it comes to pronouncements, based on the Bible, on the value of other traditions. Moreover, the religions of the ancient Near East surrounding the people of Israel, and those of ancient Rome and Greece in the period when Christianity came to birth, no longer exist. Is it legitimate, therefore, to judge what we should think in the present about religious plurality in relation to the purposes of God if we peer only through the lens of those dynamics from long ago?

However, as we know, this has not prevented biblical scholars and theologians from bending Scripture towards their specific projects or purposes in the arena of theology and interfaith relations. For, at one level, the relevance of Scripture to interfaith understanding is simply one instance of the general hermeneutical task of applying scriptural insights to modern-day realities. In a great many instances, there may be no specific answers to specific problems as these have arisen in contemporary times; nevertheless, there may be general principles which could apply.

1

For example, take the issue of stem-cell research. The Bible knows nothing of modern genetics but that need not stop us from Christian decision-making about stem-cell research based on some general interpretation of what Scripture entails. These principles could well involve the following: the dignity of individual human lives; the cure of disease by extending belief in divinely intended healing through scientific means; the wisdom of extending medical professional power over unformed human life. Yet the application of general principles in the interfaith arena seems more challenging than in relation to specific problems. To come straight to the point: 'other faiths' present alternative 'soteriological spaces' for the project called 'salvation' and they therefore present themselves, at least initially, as rival contestants for our committed attention. This lends an urgency to the question of how Scripture might be relevant to the interpretation of our multifaith world.

But it is pertinent to ask if there is such a thing as 'the biblical view' on anything – whether we are thinking of specific problems such as stem-cell research or the bigger picture of interpreting humanity's varied religious history. An older theological scholarship, which still continues today in various guises, assumed that such a view was readily available and could be constituted under the rubric of 'salvation history'. This outlook was present already in the New Testament, received its defining outline in the writings of Augustine and flowered abundantly under Protestant (and later Catholic) thought with the rise of the so-called biblical theology movement with its stress on the 'acts of God'. The basic scheme affirmed God's act of creation, lamented the fall of humanity with Adam and Eve, rejoiced in the rescue from sin with redemption won in Jesus Christ and looked forward to final consummation in the fullness of God's eschatological kingdom. God chose a people, the Israelites, to be a light to the nations, but they continually failed in their vocation until the time of Jesus whose death and resurrection inaugurated a new covenant and the age of the Church. As Oscar Cullman, a key exponent of 'salvation history', expressed it:

> Thus the entire redemptive history unfolds in two movements: the one proceeds from the many to the One; this is the Old Covenant. The other proceeds from the One to the many; this is the New Covenant. At the very mid-point stands the expiatory deed of the death and resurrection of Christ ... The Church on earth, in which the body of Christ is represented, plays in the New Testament conception a central role for the redemption of all mankind and thereby for the entire creation.[1]

God's saving activity runs as a hidden thread through history, bringing restoration out of defeat and hope out of abandonment. In this scheme the presence of other religions in the world had no place, except that the Jews and Judaism were superseded by the new people of God. It is easy to see why this whole approach remains profoundly inadequate in an age which is learning to value, or at least be open to, the spiritualities and insights of people of other traditions. But more than that, the 'biblical theology' outlook as a whole failed to explain how the activity of God in 'salvation history' related to the passage of time in 'secular history'. Furthermore,

> This whole approach remains profoundly inadequate in an age which is learning to value . . . the spiritualities and insights of people of other traditions

how the impact of critical historical thinking might relate to a scheme such as 'salvation history' was largely ignored. What was important was to work with the myth of 'salvation history' as God's story that was alive within a random world history story. It is easy to see why this 'biblical theology' outlook could not survive the rise of multifaith consciousness. Cullman's view that Jesus Christ stood in the midst of time was parochial at best.

Updating 'biblical theology'

However, the fading of the heyday of the 'biblical theology' movement has not stopped the emergence of various successors who have sought to demonstrate how the sweep of biblical literature and history might relate more positively to the prospects of Christian faith's relations with other religions. An excellent Catholic example of this can be found in the book *The Biblical Foundations for Mission*, by scholars Donald Senior and Carroll Stuhlmueller. Here is their conclusion following a magisterial account of how the biblical material understands the reality of God who is universally present to the whole world:

> The Bible gives awesome witness to the universal sovereignty of God. His lordship and provident care transcend every human boundary – even those of Israel and the church. His compassionate embrace of humanity cannot be circumscribed by our careful moral calculations. The biblical story constantly shatters the efforts of religious people to bottle up God . . . Any claim to exclusivity or religious triumphalism will eventually run aground on the expansive vision of the biblical God.[2]

For Senior and Stuhlmueller the universal presence of God in the Bible is revealed to the world in multiple ways: through diverse creation, evolving history, human experience and the insight of Israel that God's will intends the salvation of the whole world. In other words, the world is not abandoned in spite of the prevalence of evil or the wilful forgetfulness of God by human beings. The Bible has been described as 'God's love affair with his people', but within the pages of that love affair there are suggestions that God's divine concern is an unrestricted concern: it is alive with all peoples and it can be traced throughout the whole biblical literature. Scholars of this outlook are fond of citing verses which reflect this universality – for example,

4

the calling of other nations besides Israel, as in Amos 9.7: the same God who brought Israel out of Egypt brought 'the Philistines from Caphtor and the Syrians from Kir'; or the recognition of an outsider's acceptability to God in Luke's story of Peter's encounter with Cornelius: 'I truly understand that . . . in every nation anyone who fears him and does what is right is acceptable to him' (Acts 10.34–35). But it is not simply individual texts that reveal God's universal care; the whole thrust of the biblical literature is non-exclusive. Even when Israel emphasizes its vocation to be a 'light to the nations' or when the Church calls attention to the deter-minative nature of Jesus's death and resurrection there remains the acknowledgement that God has not left himself without witnesses in other places and among other peoples. In the biblical theology framework this provides permission for openness, generosity and interreligious dialogue in relation to 'others' of our own day.

> God has not left himself without witnesses in other places and among other peoples

Senior and Stuhlmueller are examples of the great flowering of biblical scholarship among Catholic theologians since Vatican II. A similar outlook also prevails among many Protestant theologians, and especially among those who had a missionary career in the twentieth century. For example, the doyen theologian of dialogue, Kenneth Cracknell, ends his survey of biblical literature as follows:

> We have suggested in this survey that all human history, from creation to end-time, in every phase and among all nations and people, must be understood as a single 'history of salvation'. Embedded in the purpose of creation is the reconciliation of all humankind to God. Now we need a way of understanding how God has communicated with humanity through all this history, and in every part of it.[3]

With both Catholic and Protestant surveys the conclusion is similar: the concept of 'biblical theology' is more or less retained but its scope extended. For our purposes, precisely how these surveys then lend themselves to a theology of religions appropriate for the emerging dialogue of our times is less clear. Cracknell slides most easily into an Inclusivist picture by folding the expansive biblical vision into the '*logos* theology' of the early Church which he sees as a direct consequence of suggestive leads in the New Testament. Senior and Stuhlmueller are slightly more guarded when they note that, in the New Testament, 'explicit evaluations of other religions tended to be negative. The Gentiles suffered from "ignorance" and were considered to be caught in a life of idolatry and futility.'[4] Nevertheless, they aver that there are biblical trajectories which can be exploited in stories and renditions of affirmation regarding God's desire for the salvation of all peoples, traces of which may be found in their religious experience, ethical conduct and evident spirituality.

Large-scale surveys of biblical material are often impressive and contain many insights which subvert assumptions that limit God's concerns narrowly to only the people of Israel and the Church, especially when carried out by careful scholars such as the ones I have mentioned. They might have avoided some of the pitfalls of older versions of 'biblical theology' by becoming more nuanced in the ways in which they interrogate the literature, but it is still fair to put the more searching question: why should patterns of faith formulated in very different times from our own, with very different assumptions about what constitutes the 'acts of God' or the flow of history, be *determinative* for the Christian response in the present? The impact of other forms of religious experience (as outlined for example in *Life of Pi* – see the Introduction) make their own claims upon us. To render other forms of experience as also examples of 'salvation history' could be a sleight of hand when based on biblical considerations alone.

Occasionally the giveaway of this arises when stories are made to yield a conclusion which is probably unwarranted. For example, in Acts 17.22–31 Luke has the Apostle Paul debating with the men of Athens on the Areopagus (Mars Hill). Should this be read as a great argumentative exchange or as a gentle interfaith dialogue? Paul has established 'points of contact' with his audience by letting the men of Athens know both that he has observed their 'altar to an unknown God' and that he agrees with the Stoic or Epicurean teachers of Greek philosophy who accepted that 'In him (God) we live and move and have our being' (v. 28). He agrees with them that God does not reside in gold or silver or stone. But when he announces the purpose of all religious affiliation ('salvation history') as defined and clarified by that declared in the death and resurrection of Christ then the men of Athens either scoff at him or walk away from the encounter. Commentators such as Cracknell, who are inclined towards an optimistic assessment of the story for inclusive 'salvation history' purposes, write that 'Luke was showing us a method for the sharing [of] the Gospel across cultural boundaries',[5] where the dispute is best envisaged as a discussion/dialogue among wise people. The alternative – and to me, more likely – reading is that Luke was interested in the spiritual life of the Athenians with the express desire of winning them over to the Christian message. Therefore Paul is depicted not so much as in a dialogue in the present-day sense of sharing experiences and learning mutually from one another, but as laying out a strategy for conversion emboldened by the superiority of the Christian message.[6]

Does this mean that our present-day context has nothing to learn from biblical scholarship? By no means, and it would be odd to suggest so. Yet perhaps a method of using the Bible for Christian reflection on plurality should be less direct. We enter

the strange world of the New Testament prepared to comprehend with all the historical tools of research available to us the
nature of that early Christian context, the reasons for the shape
of the New Testament witness (together with that of the Hebrew
Scriptures), and so on, and then return to our own day ready to
face new questions in new times and in wholly different circumstances. What we bring with us is bound to be less directly applic-
able than perhaps we would wish. But at least we will not be
pressing our present experiences
into solutions devised for different circumstances, no matter how
'holy' we deem 'Scripture' to be.
As the Finnish New Testament
scholar, Heikki Räisänen, has
said: 'The exegete may be needed in the global village as the
"historical conscience" in the dialogue, as one who warns of
attempts to make too direct a use of the texts.'[7]

> The exegete may be needed in the global village ... as one who warns of attempts to make too direct a use of the texts

Those who rely on 'biblical theology' have at least two broad
areas of potential misunderstanding to clarify for any contemporary interpretation of religious pluralism to be convincing.
The first is what to say about the category of idolatry, which is
a constant bedrock complaint about 'other religions' throughout the Bible; and the second is how to interpret the so-called
difficult verses which have been appropriated for polemical purposes against other religions down the ages. Let me say a brief
word about each of these issues, before drawing the discussion
to a close.

Idolatry

It is abundantly clear that biblical religion is opposed to idolatry.
The source of this prohibition is the monotheistic belief
that 'God' is beyond compare. The prohibition is there in the

founding story of Moses receiving the Ten Commandments, the second of which is, 'You shall not make for yourself an idol . . .' (Exodus 20.4). Islam of course is well-known for its similar strong prohibition on idols, 'association' of material things with Allah (*shirk*) being perhaps the greatest of human faults. Christian tradition too has a strong aversion to idol worship, an attitude inherited from Judaism. However, Christianity has been more prepared than its Abrahamic siblings to develop a theology of symbolism in terms of sacraments and the role of images/icons, developments which even now for some Protestant Christians, however, come close to idolatry. The transcendent otherness of the divine should not be impugned.

The Greco-Roman world in which Christian faith came to birth was infused with idol worship. Pagan cultic worship, local festivals, gatherings of trade guilds all involved a citizen in idol worship. Jews were known to separate themselves from such practices, but they were tolerated, especially as they had historical venerability in their favour. But what of the Christians, and particularly what of the Gentile Christians? Would their conversion entail a pulling away from attendance at festivals or guild meetings and thereby arouse the suspicion of the pagan world? Would becoming Christian therefore entail withdrawal from civic life and thus affect a person's social standing or prospects of employment?

It turns out that while the general prohibition against idolatry was maintained as a bottom line in Christian circles there were also different approaches to it. The Apostle Paul, who is our main source for this, in fact can be ambivalent. The issue comes to a head over the issue of eating meat which has been offered to idols. Are Christians allowed to eat this meat? The answers range from 'Yes', because the idols are really worthless in terms of the gods they portray for these gods do not exist, to 'No', because those Christians who imagine that these gods do exist would be scandalized and Christian solidarity is a higher value than fraternizing with pagans. Moreover, the issue was not simply theoretical belief – do the gods exist or don't they? – but the association between either idol worship and moral depravity, the cultic dabbling with evil spirits, or the linking of cultic worship with the Emperor and the oppressive Empire.

Numerous factors therefore strengthened the prohibition on idols. Modern differentiations between religious, social, ethical and political dimensions of life would not have been possible in the ancient world. On the whole, Paul's attitude was liberal in the context of his time: it was possible to eat the meat unless there were good reasons not to. In pastoral practice then, for Paul, there is a combination of free choice, ambivalent uncertainty, and perhaps sheer prejudice in his responses to idolatry and its implications. As the first century progressed a narrowing of attitude and exclusivist tendencies began to prevail.

What seem like related issues arise also in the modern context. When Christians visit a Hindu temple in a modern Western city should they receive the *prasad* which is often offered to visitors? Although *prasad* (sacred food) does not have the connotation of, say, the eucharistic bread of Christian worship, a question of religious identity arises. Some Christians in the West decline to receive the *prasad* out of solidarity with Christian friends in India, where the Christian church is a small minority and is constantly alert to the possibility that it may lose its specific identity in a dominant Hindu setting which potentially embraces all religious expressions under an inclusive umbrella. But Christians in the West are more likely to receive the *prasad* simply as a sign of hospitality and friendship with their Hindu neighbours. Does eating the *prasad* associate one with 'idolatry', however unwittingly, as practised in Hindu temples?

Actually, the deeper question is whether or not Christians have understood the nature of 'idolatry' as a religious practice.

10

This is not a matter of whether or not the gods depicted in, say, Hindu temples exist, ontologically as it were or as part of a vast polytheistic panoply, but whether or not we have taken the time to comprehend how images, idols, 'wood and stone' function within the religious matrix of worship. Christian missionaries were often involved in wholesale misrepresentation, as in the well-known hymn (though largely omitted now from hymn collections) by Bishop Reginald Heber of Calcutta (1783–1826), containing the line 'The heathen in his blindness bows down to wood and stone.'

Idolatry has been a source of suspicion in relation to indigenous religions, so-called nature religions, and certain Eastern expressions of religiousness, such as Buddhism as well as Hinduism. But how do we interpret idolatry? Did those missionaries grasp the significance of idols aright? Wilfred Cantwell Smith has written:

> Christian (and Jewish) failure to understand, let alone to appreciate, what is going on in the spiritual life of communities served by images, is integral to the Bible, and to our tradition. Indeed, the error was a failure to recognize that anything at all was going on spiritually. As a result, the concepts developed have signified the material objects involved but have omitted the transcendent dimension that was their primary significance.[8]

To mistake the materially obvious for the mysteriously transcendent is the essence of idolatry. But that is not what is happening in what Westerners have pejoratively called idolatry.

Take Hinduism, for instance. It is not the case that Hindus bow down to wood and stone *per se* but to the divinity which is evoked by them, and which they depict in their characteristic subjects (e.g. Krishna playing his flute with his consort Radha beside him). In a Hindu temple, when the curtains surrounding the *murti* (the proper term for what Westerners have frequently misunderstood as idols) are pulled back at the

11

beginning of acts of temple worship, what is being configured is a symbolic sacred universe whereby the devotees gaze on the divine as construed through certain forms and the divine gazes on the devotee. This is *darshan*, a divine seeing. Of course, it relies on a whole theology of how God relates to the world in a Hindu worldview if we are to understand *darshan* fully in its own terms. Something similar could be said about the Christian approach to the eucharistic bread and wine – a theory of sacramental symbolism lies behind the 'naming' of material bread and wine as Christ's body and blood.

Idolatry is the worship of that which is not-God as God. This is why the main problem in the Exodus story of Moses presenting the Ten Commandments to the people is the worship of wealth – the calf was golden! Idolatry in its true sense is the substitution of the infinite transcendent power and authority which is God by other objects which are merely finite but yet have acquired an equivalent transcendent status. Whom or What we serve, in terms of the things we take with unconditional seriousness, is a pertinent question – and it extends to the worldly realities of power, wealth, militarism, political ideology, and so on. Might it also be possible for the Christian Church to confuse its conception of God with God *per se*? Some have said that insistence on 'one way' or 'one truth' can be a form of idolatry, imagining a human product as a divine fact. Again, as Wilfred Cantwell Smith has observed:

> Christians have been wrong in thinking that Hindus are formally idolaters. We would do well, on the other hand, to recognize that we Christians have substantially been idolaters, insofar as we have mistaken for God, or as universally final, the particular forms of Christian life or thought.[9]

Pretence in claiming to know final truth is precisely that, pretence – a form of idolatry.

If the 'wood and stone' accompaniments of religious worship lure us into false consciousness and false security then they are to be shunned in the name of the God of transcendent consciousness. On the other hand, if they are an aid to the worship of the God of transcendent goodness, mercy and compassion, then they deserve a more subtle treatment than has usually prevailed in Christian history.

Difficult verses

Let me turn now to one of the most difficult if also misunderstood and misapplied verses of the New Testament in Christian reflection on other religions. This is the verse from John's Gospel:

> Jesus said to him [Thomas], 'I am the way, the truth and the life. No-one comes to the Father except through me.' (John 14.6)

How are we to think of this verse, so often used as clear evidence that a proper Christian stance before other traditions ought to be an exclusivistic one? Kenneth Cracknell has set out a long exposition of this verse and its immediate context in John and claims that it is expressive of the very opposite of what a surface reading would suggest. Jesus' reply to Thomas is a reply to a question about how to discern the real intention and purpose of Jesus' forthcoming journey – his way – to the cross. As Cracknell says: 'Thomas in our view is asking, "Lord what is your ultimate intention, and how do we follow you in achieving so great a purpose?"'[10] It is the demonstration of the cross which will declare God the Father's act of reconciliation for the world and it is this which is in view, not the business of the acceptability of other faith traditions. Cracknell does, however, go on to elaborate a *logos* theology, whereby the manifestation of divine will, intention and being is more clearly set forth in Jesus as 'the word made flesh' than in other ways, yet without the dismissing or denigration of these other ways. Whether or not this theology is adequate for our own day is a moot point and I shall look at this in the next chapter.

I could have selected other 'difficult verses' (e.g. Acts 4.12: 'There is salvation in no one else, for there is no other name under heaven given among mortals by which we must be saved') for consideration, but let me stay with my own response to this infamous Johannine verse and set out a number of points which can therefore function as a kind of case study of what an indirect application of one biblical passage might look like. My points are these:

1 It is unlikely that Jesus ever uttered these words. They come in John's Gospel, which is generally reckoned to contain few words of Jesus himself and is best read as an extended meditation on the meaning of Jesus for the world (though it is likely that there will be some historical material retained within it). Therefore the words of 14.6 cannot be used as a kind of dominical trump card in a game of comparative competition between religions.

2 'I am the way, the truth and the life' is one of a number of recognized 'I am' sayings in John's Gospel – comparable to 'I am the light of the world', 'I am the door', 'I am the resurrection', and so on. These sayings are metaphorically accredited to Jesus to indicate how it is that he provides mediation between heaven and earth, God and the world. They are titles placed on the lips of Jesus as interpretations of his role and status in being an occasion for disclosure about God's intentions for the world.

3 'Way, truth and life' sits alongside the identifying of Jesus as the *logos* of God, the background to which is more Jewish than many older commentaries assumed. So John's prologue likely echoes Isaiah which says that 'the word of God goes

14

forth . . .' and the Book of Proverbs where 'wisdom' is imagined in personified form as a master workman beside God
from the beginning of creation. Jesus was identified with these
images – Word, Wisdom – as a way of expressing the conviction that as a result of him the transformation envisaged
through God's purposes for the world was all-encompassing.
Something similar is at work in John 14.6. Jesus as the *logos*
is related to the Father as a son: he is a 'chip off the old block',
reproducing in his human impact the essential characteristics
of his divine Father. We are in the realms of poetry and not
metaphysics, metaphor and not realism.

4 The metaphors 'way', 'truth' and 'life' form a single whole and
affirm the same value in different words. They are hugely
resonant in John's theology, which interprets Jesus as God's
revelatory communication with the world. Their essential
burden is to indicate that Jesus is genuine for the purposes
for which he exists. In other words, in him what is encountered is authentic and not a fake. The word for 'truth' (*aletheia*)
in John's lectionary generally translates as 'genuine'. It is not
a comparative term in relation to other 'ways' as abstract
'truths'. Positively, the bundle of metaphors in 14.6 is affirming
that the character, intention and heart of God are authentically manifest in this figure of Jesus. Negatively, however, they
indicate nothing about the genuineness of other 'ways'.
They can be judged on their own merits.

5 The verse can be compared to the personal appreciation that
'my partner is the most beautiful person in the world'. In other
words, it celebrates everything positive about 'partner' but says
nothing about other loving relationships in other partnerships.

6 In John's Gospel 'Jesus' replaces Judaism and Judaism's
religious mediations for approaching the mysterious reality
of God. So the Torah, Temple and sacrifice were all replaced
by Jesus the divine Word who precedes even the prophets

as mediators of divine graciousness and demand. For some Jewish commentators it was Torah that was held in the bosom of 'the Father' as 'the way, truth and life' before it was given on earth through Moses. For John, Jesus now displaces the Torah in this role of mediation. Again we are dealing with poetry. But it is poetry with a bite. The displacement forms part of John's anti-Judaism and reflects the emerging Jewish-Christian 'parting of the ways' at the end of the first century.

What is the upshot of my six points? The application of contextual and historical analysis does not allow us to pluck John 14.6 from its context in the whole Gospel as a solution to problems in the Christian theology of religions and to do so is to misconstrue John's Gospel. We do the Bible a disservice if we take texts designed for one period and turn them into filters for solving other problems in later periods. To this extent, John 14.6 has nothing whatsoever to do with the Christian theology of religions. However, there is one sense in which it reflects a theology of religious concern, and that is in its origins in Jewish–Christian dispute. It is part of emerging Christian supersessionism over Judaism (the view that Judaism is destined to fade away in the light of the new Christian revelation) and as such ought to be treated with grave caution. For the most part, the official mainline churches and the mainstream theological world have given up on supersessionism. This is largely due to Christian responses to the Holocaust, to the persistence of Judaism as a vital tradition and to theological belief in the binding promises of God to the Jewish people. In other words, and almost in spite of what many would see as the general thrust of New Testament texts such as John 14.6, the theological world has not followed John at this crucial point.

> **John 14.6 has nothing whatsoever to do with the Christian theology of religions**

Many factors are at work in a contemporary theology of religions. My excursion into John 14.6 has I hope demonstrated how indirect the application of biblical texts might be in fashioning such a theology. Moreover, a central question when reflecting on the use of biblical material for theology of religions is: to what extent should the emerging Church, separating itself from first-century Judaism over the years following the Roman destruction of the Jerusalem Temple in 70 CE, be a template for deciding the Christian view of religious plurality today? Senior and Stuhlmueller offer the following remarks at the end of their study:

> Any solution on the part of Christians that can only see the church as the complete fulfillment of the promises to Israel and therefore considers Judaism to be an anachronistic and discarded prototype is incompatible with the Bible and with the facts of history . . . To treat Jews as one more non-Christian religion and to embark on a strategy of individual conversion is not in the spirit of the Bible and is to be too sure of a question that the biblical people hesitated to answer.[11]

Judaism is not 'other religions', and furthermore, biblical Judaism is not what rabbinical Judaism evolved into. It is often said that Judaism and Christianity are two religions who share a common ancestor in pre-rabbinic and pre-Christian biblical literature. If that is so, then the biblical material is even more indirect in its bearing on how Christians should think about other religions.[12]

2

Between Exclusivist-Repudiation and Inclusivist-Toleration

Tension from the beginning

The scriptures of a tradition inevitably celebrate the truth of what has been given or glimpsed through experience and recorded within their pages. They confirm identity and give shape to the meaning of religious commitment for those who take them to heart. In other words, scriptures become a foundational reference by encapsulating a tradition's origins and/or unfolding a story over time. In one major sense, therefore, they reflect insider truth and what remains is the challenge to interpret them wisely for those who live by them.

But scriptures are rarely consistent and this can be illustrated with reference to a saying that occurs in both Mark's and Matthew's Gospel, and which will lead us into the theological discussion of this chapter.

In Mark's Gospel (overwhelmingly accepted as the earliest of the four Gospels and dated to about 70 CE), the disciple John, brother of James, tells Jesus that he tried to prevent someone who was outside the official circle of disciples from performing a healing miracle using the name of Jesus. The response of Jesus is to rebuke John severely and he summarizes his teaching with the saying: 'Whoever is not against us is for us' (Mark 9.40).

The business of enacting God's kingdom of love and justice, it seems, is not confined to the official disciple group. When Matthew copied Mark's Gospel some 10 to 20 years later, the saying was altered in order to serve a wholly different purpose: 'Whoever is not with me is against me' (Matthew 12.30).

This more-or-less reversal is in line with Matthew's general disposition, which is to firm up boundaries where Mark had left them open. Matthew places the saying in a setting where Jesus is the cause of division between the Pharisees, who are depicted as being on the side of Satan (and therefore blaspheme against the divine Spirit), and Jesus and his followers, who represent the coming kingdom of God. For Mark, Jesus' rebuke arises out of a misperception by the disciples, who therefore require correction; for Matthew it is the Pharisees who are the culprits and who require repudiation with a rephrased saying.

The tension between Mark's 'misperception-needing-correction' and Matthew's 'conflict-requiring-repudiation' in relation to those outside the official circle of disciples can be an intriguing lens through which to view the Christian reaction to other religions over its long history. Does the message of healing/salvation, through the impact of God's kingdom at work in Jesus, involve us in a Marcan-type *inclusive collaboration with* or a Matthean-type *exclusive rejection of* outsiders?

In 1983 I published the book *Christians and Religious Pluralism*,[1] in which I explored the theology of religions under the typological headings Exclusivism, Inclusivism and Pluralism, and many have found them illuminating as a framework for approaching Christian responses to other religions. Since then the discussion has spun off in many directions and the adequacy of these categories has been questioned, either because they restrict the real responses of Christians to other religions too tightly or because this whole approach is said to be misconstrued and involves some kind of category mistake. While the business of interfaith relations has changed dramatically during the intervening period, however, I see no reason to abandon the categories. I shall address in this and the next chapters the concerns others have expressed about them,[2] believing that the original three-fold typology simply describes the available logical avenues of thought. These are:

- Christ is the only source of transcendent transformation (Exclusivism);
- Christ is the most complete of the religious choices on offer regarding transcendent transformation (Inclusivism);
- Christ is one of a possible number of sources of transcendent transformation (Pluralism).

This chapter considers Exclusivism and Inclusivism as a pairing of options, both of which retain a hold on Christian absolutism. In the next chapter I shall outline a theology of Pluralism but do so in conjunction with its main antagonist, which is sometimes termed 'Particularism'. This latter considers the various religious pathways to be so different in their orientations that it is not even possible to approach the issue of whether or not other religions bear salvific potency, for there is simply no way of knowing what an answer might look like. I consider pairing Particularism with Pluralism because the latter represents the arch-heretical spectre against which Particularists fulminate.

Occasionally the theology of religions is framed in terms of a choice between the specificity of a tradition and the universalism to which it points. One is said to be either specific by being rooted in tradition or universalist by being free to discern the divine presence wherever it may be intuited. Put like that, this is a false distinction. All religious traditions discern the universal presence of God (ultimate reality) through the matrix of their specific traditions. By being specific, one is universal in outlook. The theology of religions question arises when different universal visions, stemming from different specific experiences and histories, encounter one another. Do we correct any misperception that the divine cannot be found outside the

Christian compound or do we repudiate the tradition that is different simply because it is different?

With this question in mind, let me now turn to the Exclusivist and Inclusivist theologies proper.

Exclusivist-Repudiation

The middle years of twentieth-century theology were dominated by European continental theologians (e.g. Karl Barth, Emil Brunner, Hendrik Kraemer), giants whose general assumption was that Christian faith is *sui generis*, that is, in a category of its own kind. The phenomenology of religions might investigate the outworkings of Christianity in terms of its beliefs, practices, cult, architecture and so on, and place these alongside the cultural products of other traditions, but this exercise in comparative phenomenology could not yield results which contributed towards the theological assessment of the world religions. In Christ, God had communicated with the world in a manner which was unlike any other. Let the following quotation from the Dutch missionary, J. H. Bavinck (1895–1964), contemporary with the continental giants, illustrate the point:

> The real Christ differs radically from the so-called saviours conjured up by the religions of man (*sic*). His gospel is not the answer to man's inquiry, but in a deep and profound sense the gospel of Christ is rather a condemnation of all such human fancy and speculation.[3]

For this school of Christian thought there is all the difference between what we term, on the one hand, 'the religions' and, on the other, 'Christian revelation'. A great gulf between them is fixed. If we ask how such a gulf exists, given orthodox Christian belief in the unity of God's world and the presumed presence of God 'to' and 'for' the world, the answer is that the Christian revelation's sense of its own unique worth is guaranteed by God's own decree, by the giving of himself in Jesus Christ, by Scripture's words of witness and by the preaching of the Church. God is not answerable to anything outside Godself and does not require justification at the bar of reason or comparative religion. Two generations ago Emil Brunner (1889–1966), the Swiss Calvinist, expressed it like this, in terms less confrontational sounding than Bavinck's:

> The world with a million fingers points toward God, but it cannot reveal Him to us ... That God exists is testified by reason, conscience and nature with its wonders. But who God is – God Himself must tell us in His revelation.[4]

And in the present generation Daniel Strange puts it more abstractly while adding a further twist regarding Scripture:

> both the self-attesting, personal and ultimate authority of divine revelation is what it is solely because it is derived from a God who is self-attesting, personal and absolute.[5]

and

> there is an ontological relationship between God and his words.[6]

What are we to make of these kinds of affirmations? It seems hard to escape the impression that they occupy a world of their own knowing, a top-down model which is independent of any encounter let alone serious dialogue with others. In a bid to secure the absolute uniqueness of the Christian revelation and all the authorities which underpin it – in Scripture, in Christ, in doctrines, in the Church – this Exclusivist rationale is placed on a 'self-attesting' basis, which amounts to being placed beyond criticism. Scripture's truth is what it is because God determines it so. That is the import of Strange's twist, that God has words to impart and whatever God imparts springs from God's very

22

being. With that assumption in play it is a logical deduction that other different words from other different religions must necessarily originate from a source other than God.

But we are surely at liberty to enquire further about such a privileged sense of knowing, otherwise we are bordering on a gnosticism at odds with critical thinking on any level. It seems impossible to escape the response that the self-attesting view in relation to Scripture necessarily requires belief in verbal inerrancy, as well as the turning of a blind eye to the pluriform content of Scripture itself.

The issue of verbal inerrancy raises a different discussion in its own right. Given that one of the prime goals of verbal inspiration is to absolve God of inconsistency of being and behaviour it is small wonder that the issue comes to the fore also in the Exclusivist theology of religions view. However, inerrancy seems an unlikely candidate to uphold in the light of criticism. Think, for example, of the tension between Mark and Matthew with which this chapter began. (It is no accident that Strange cites Matthew's confrontational either-or account as containing Jesus' authentic words and not Mark!) If that tension is beside the point then the abstract nature of the claim regarding the inviolability of Scripture becomes all the more obscure.

But there is a bigger problem than any doctrine of inerrancy. Scripture requires interpretation and whose interpretation will we take? What can the claim that there is an 'ontological relationship between God and his words' really mean? It goes beyond even the earlier 'biblical theology' approach explored in the previous chapter. This would render the biblical words divine, but even on orthodox grounds this has never been an acceptable theological viewpoint. In hermeneutical times, such as our own, this strikes us as being an attempt to bypass any critical judgements about the nature of the text and the role of human interpreters seeking to bring texts to life for later times.

Scripture records a people's experience over many centuries and it is clear within the text that reflection on that experience is bounded by time and place: human beings can only speak in the tones and sounds of their contextual placing.

Finally, in relation to the negative judgement about other religions, Exclusivist-Repudiation considers that we know what to think about others in advance of our encounter with them. This seems to me to be either arrogance or a refusal to acknowledge that the experienced realities of the world have any bearing whatsoever on how we are to interpret the facts of religious plurality. And this is just odd.

> **Exclusivist-Repudiation considers that we know what to think about others in advance of our encounter with them**

That last statement could be said to carry the critique too far, for many Exclusivist-Repudiationists also affirm some sense of the presence of God in and to the world through a notion of general revelation, an echo of God's presence in nature, conscience, reason and cultural experience. For this group, God is never absent from the world, a perspective which also has biblical resonance, as we saw in the last chapter. Yet – and it is a highly charged 'yet' – for Exclusivist-Repudiationists, any knowledge, intuition or suggestion of God cannot stand on its own independent terms, for the 'self-attesting' sovereignty of God outlaws such a possibility. Therefore any knowledge of God from general revelation turns out to be, to cite Brunner again, 'like stammering words from some half-forgotten saying.'[7] A fairly negative judgement indeed!

The problem for Exclusivist-Repudiationists is that both Scripture and experiential encounter attest to a sense of spiritual awareness outside the Christian witness to it. The equally Exclusivist Dutch Protestant, Hendrik Kraemer (1888–1965), recognized this when he wrote:

Our verdict on the religions – that 'in their deepest and most essential meaning and purpose' they are *in error* – must be firmly maintained, as I see it; but to be fair (and even to be correct) we must, I think, balance that by saying with equal emphasis and conviction that despite that fundamental failing the religions constitute a field of human endeavour in which, yes, even at the very heart of 'error' itself, we are to discover and to recognise that 'God has passed this way'.[8]

Kraemer seeks balance, but it is clear that even if 'God has passed this way' God does not linger for long. So how do Kraemer and others interpret that divine 'passing'? What is the connection between the divine 'passing' and the human practice of religious commitment in other traditions? Is the legacy of divine involvement with other traditions positive or negative? For Kraemer and his successors, the answer has to be overwhelmingly negative.

Let me explain further. The Exclusivist-Repudiationist's 'No' judgement is often said to derive from the overall momentum of Christian Scripture. But in fact it usually stems from a selective use of Scripture. Of importance to many Exclusivist-Repudiationists, for example, is the passage from Romans where the Apostle Paul says, in 1.18–32, that there is a real knowledge of God available through the created order, knowledge of 'God's eternal power and divine nature', but it has become distorted and is entangled with idolatry. Therefore any effective knowledge of God outside the prism of Jesus Christ is both pure illusion and actively perverse.

The theologian Bavinck, cited earlier, says of this passage that while there is a genuine revelation of God in the world apart from that in Jesus Christ it is so distorted as to be not only worthless but also culpable. Because of human sinfulness it is 'suppressed' and 'exchanged' for an idolatrous counterfeit. What this means is that not only is it impossible for the natural human mind to comprehend God through general revelation, as a function of straightforward human knowing, but it is also impossible for us to know that we don't know authentically. The visible consequence is idolatry, attachment to misappropriated material representations of God, the result of our perverted human condition.

What God gives through general revelation, human beings misconstrue and distort through their sinfulness; we are humanly incapable of perceiving and knowing aright. For this reason Kraemer called other religions a 'dark excursion of the mind'.[9]

What is the bearing of this on religious plurality? Even if this Bavinck–Kraemer–Brunner–Strange type analysis is convincing, though it does seem contorted to say the least, how do its supporters apply it to the impact of religious plurality? The answer is by equating 'the religions' of the world with the ancient Roman and Greek religions, which made extensive use of idols. Yet this seems strangely perverted itself, for what really amounts to a localized contextual issue for Paul in Rome (and other cities of the ancient world) is extrapolated into a general principle for every time and place. Yet surely this is wholly unwarranted. The repudiation of Greco-Roman idolatry provides no mandate for relations with other religions more generally. How can it apply to Judaism and Islam, Christianity's Abrahamic siblings, who are equally, if not more, adamant about the dangers of idolatry? And in relation to other traditions (e.g. Buddhism and Hinduism), I have already commented on why we should aim to comprehend the nature of idol worship much better than we do (see pp. 8–13).

For Exclusivist-Repudiationists the impact of our dawning awareness of religious plurality is negligible. The 'unsaved' mind fails to know God's purpose or nature because it lies outside the knowledge of God as disclosed in Jesus Christ. Any knowledge of God through non-Christian means is either impossible or so distorted that it convicts us of wilful depraved idolatry: those who are not with us are against us. There can be no breaching of the absoluteness of Jesus Christ.

Let me turn now to a second style of approach to the question of other religions, which is a modified form of Christian absolutism.

Inclusivist-Toleration

It is sometimes assumed that Christian theology until recent times has always been negative about other religions. This is a wrong assumption, as the following citation from the second-century Christian writer, Justin Martyr, shows:

> We are taught that Christ is the first-born of God, and . . . he is the Word of whom all humanity has a share, and those who lived according to the Logos [*hoi meta logou biosantes*] are therefore Christians, even though they were regarded as atheists; among Greeks, Socrates, and Heraclitus; and among non-Greeks, Abraham, Ananias, Azanus, and Misad, and Elias, and many others.[10]

At one level this seems a highly paradoxical thing to say. Yet for many theologians of the first centuries it was a standard formulation, as it helped to answer the puzzling question of what God was up to in relation to the salvation of those good people who lived before the advent of Jesus Christ. God was always present! It represents an insight which has lived on through Christian history and has been extended by modern theologians to apply also to those after Christ who have never heard of him, or who might have heard but in a manner which has been less than existentially convincing. In fact, it is probably safe to say that this represents the dominant approach to people of other traditions since the second half of the twentieth century.

27

But how can Socrates, for example, be called a Christian before Jesus ever lived? The answer lies in the *logos* theology of the early church theologians. The *logos* was the divine principle of rationality which lay within the intelligibility of the world. It indicated reason, purpose and creativity, all features of experience which characterize human beings and link us with God's rational purpose. *Logos* was the means by which men and women participated in the reason of God and, moreover, in the person of Jesus, this participation was uniquely embodied and expressed. Jesus was *logos* incarnate (enfleshed), or God's very self somehow portrayed in human terms. By virtue of this doctrine of incarnation all those who 'lived according to the *logos*' lived according to the same principle that was fully operative in Jesus Christ. Therefore, in some sense, that animating principle which shaped the life and work of Jesus Christ was connected to the same *logos* which was responsible for the spiritual wisdom, moral aspiration and concern for intelligibility that preoccupied many Greek philosophers.

In the same way that the Judaism of the Hebrew Bible, and especially Israel's prophetic history, was interpreted by early Christian thought as a preparation for the coming of Jesus of Nazareth as Messiah, so God was preparing the Gentiles for the coming of the *logos* incarnate, Jesus the Word. Both strategies – in relation to Greeks and Hebrews – reflect the continuity of God's presence to the world with a sense of fulfilment, summation and 'crowning' in Christ. This 'crowning' was simultaneously the cause of salvation throughout the whole world and the whole of time. Religious geography and history cohered in this one pivotal person and moment.

For my theological purposes here the *logos* theology represents a habit of mind which is prepared to respond creatively to the experience of goodness, truth and beauty outside the Christian fold. It was quintessentially summed up by the Vatican II document, *Nostra Aetate*:

The Catholic Church rejects nothing of what is true and holy in these religions. She has a high regard for the manner of life and conduct, the precepts and doctrines which, although differing in many ways from her own teaching, nevertheless often reflect a ray of that truth which enlightens all men.[11]

Yet what was given with one hand was then taken back with the other:

Yet she [the Catholic Church] proclaims ... Christ who is the way, the truth, and the life (Jn. 14.6). In him, in whom God reconciled all things to himself (2 Cor. 5.18f.), men find the fullness of their religious life.[12]

It is as though the positive recognition of other traditions, which both the study of religious history and present-day personal encounters have learned to value, is acknowledged but then trumped by the weight of theological tradition. That which is perceived to stem from the universal *logos* is essentially tolerated until such time as the full clarity of Christian saving truth can be appropriated by non-Christian believers. In this way, Inclusivist-Tolerationists seek to solve the issue of how God's presence throughout time and space coheres with that same presence in the person of Jesus the saviour, yet without the negativity redolent of the Exclusivist-Repudiationist. That cohering, however, consists in a fulfilment theory whereby Jesus Christ 'fulfils' or 'completes' the 'preparatory truths' of other ways. *Logos* theology remains tolerant of other ways and seeks to fold positive religious experience from elsewhere into a developing understanding.

It is important to clarify what I mean by the term 'tolerant'. When I say 'tolerant' of other ways this is intended to indicate the structural relationship of other religions to Christian faith and not the personal attitudes of Christians or Christian theologians towards people of other traditions. Toleration is essentially a 'putting-up-with' strategy, a provisional arrangement which ideally one would not wish to perpetuate: 'putting-up-with' is conditional on a future time when that which is inadequate would be supplanted by something much improved. For Inclusivist-Tolerationists, following the advent of Jesus Christ the religious truths, intuitions, insights of other traditions are gathered up into a revelation which represents the climax of salvation history worldwide. Other religions are 'tolerated' as movements on the way to a more all-encompassing vision. The 'toleration' as such could be either positive or negative in terms of personal attitudes, respect and the encounters between people; and it is even possible, moreover, to learn from those who are tolerated. But Inclusivist-Tolerationists assume Christian faith to be finally supreme among religions. The Catholic document *Dominus Iesus* (2000), which dauntingly characterized other religions as 'gravely deficient'[13] in respect of their salvific potency, has not been widely celebrated even among many Inclusivist-Tolerationists. It does represent, however, an accurate portrayal from the point of view of this theological approach.

A pivotal role in developing and promoting an Inclusivist vision was played by the theologian Karl Rahner (1904–84), for whom God's spirit is 'always and everywhere and in every person as the innermost center of his existence'.[14] Rahner's advance on Vatican II was that he provided for the role of history and culture in religious commitment. If God is present to all people, as he insisted was the case, then God is so by virtue of the historical means available to a person, that is, by the embodied historical experience developed according to that person's religion.

> Rahner coined the phrase 'anonymous Christian' to describe a Hindu or a Muslim or a Sikh who exists already in a saving relationship to God

To this end, Rahner coined the phrase 'anonymous Christian' to describe a Hindu or a Muslim or a Sikh, and so on, who exists already in a saving relationship to God without Jesus. Human beings are not wholly spiritual creatures but those whose lives are shaped by the contextual institutions and historical circumstances of cultural life.

Rahner's term 'anonymous Christian' has not caught on, even among Inclusivist-Tolerationists. But the general task of accepting a positive role for the religions *qua* religions has been firmly welcomed. If you ask what then about Christ and his effect, Rahner, and others since, would reply that Christ is to the other traditions as the source of light is to the rays of light; the explicit must supersede the anonymous. Hence 'toleration', until the greater light of truth can be glimpsed, received and existentially established.

From the point of view of this book the question which hovers over Inclusivist-Tolerationist types of approach is precisely how the reconciliation between God and the estranged world, which the historical figure of Jesus of Nazareth is said to have brought about by his saving work in ministry, on the cross and through the resurrection, has an effect before and after his lifetime, among those who have not heard the message. What it means for a Mahayana Buddhist or an Advaita Vedantist Hindu or a Sufi Muslim to be saved 'anonymously' through Jesus Christ seems rather obscure to many people. Furthermore, conjuring up talk of *logos* seems only to deepen the obscurity rather than illuminate an argument. *Logos* was a philosophical principle, part of a metaphysical scheme of thinking in the early centuries but sounding rather mythological in tone now. Jesus Christ was a person proclaiming and acting out the kingdom of God in history.

For these reasons some Inclusivist theologians have turned to a theology of the Spirit as a means of making more plausible intellectually the connections between what appeared in Jesus and what is alive in other traditions. It is through God's Spirit that other religions provide contexts of 'saving grace', and the movement of God's Spirit seems a more free-wheeling idea, less anchored in the 'awkward limited history' of the Jesus figure. The Spirit is that 'face' of God which blows where it wills, animating the whole of life from within, seeking a home in the hearts of all who profess openness to the possibilities of tran-scendence. Spirit language speaks of relationship, connection, a quality of interaction between centres of freedom. In this sense the presence of Spirit is unlimited throughout the world. If there is evidence of human transformation, of active loving service of others, of serious ethical endeavour and piety among the religions then the Spirit must be active.[15]

Still, the theological question persists: what is the relationship between perceived active spirit within the world's religions and the activity of the same spirit in Christian faith? For those inclusive-minded theologians who embrace readily the language of spirit the answer is that the Spirit of God in Christian terms is always the Spirit of Jesus Christ. That which is alive and present in other traditions is known and received in Christianity somehow more fully, more definitively. In other words, the puzzle of how the historic effects of the saving-Spirit-impact of Jesus of Nazareth extend to others anonymously, hiddenly or inchoately remains.

A final strategy has emerged among Inclusivist-Tolerationists for squaring the circle between Christian-specific criteria and the theologically motivated desire to honour the independent spirituality of other traditions, and this is to value the religions as movements in history as such (and therefore argue for their continuation) but postpone the confrontation of followers with Christ until the time of a person's death. Assuming even that sense can be made of such a notion, any meaning which can be attached to an encounter like this seems rather opaque. If Buddhists, Muslims and Sikhs are not completely wrong, as this view maintains, then what is the remainder of wrong which needs correction and completion in the Christian way? Welcoming other religions as part of God's providential purpose affirms people inspired and shaped by those traditions, but the imposition of Christ as universal saviour at the point of death seems like bad faith even though it is thought necessary in order to safeguard an inviolable principle that Christ is the origin of all salvation. If those of other religions do not relish being called

> The imposition of Christ as universal saviour at the point of death seems like bad faith

'Christians outside Christ' or people pursuing a 'baptism of desire' or those undergoing 'preparation for a final fulfilment', it is hard to imagine what 'turning to Christ at the time of death' might mean as well. If so, perhaps it is time for the principle itself to undergo further modification in the light of the persistence of the world religions.

Inclusivist-Toleration represents a stretching of the dynamic impact of that saving grace which erupted through the event of Jesus of Nazareth to other traditions. But it remains a top-down approach which seeks to maintain the orthodox Christian framework intact while acknowledging the effectiveness of other religions as contexts of salvific potential. But that effectiveness will always be a lesser effectiveness than the revelation in Christ – not lesser as a result of comparing the spiritual results of different traditions but lesser by the sheer fact that the priority of Christ stands as a given in the Inclusivist theological schema. To this extent it remains an *a priori* approach and shares this principle with Exclusivist-Repudiation.

Are there other ways by which we might honour the new lived information from other religions as part of a Christian outlook? We turn in the next chapter to consider a more controversial hypothesis, in conjunction with its critics, to see if such an approach can be discerned.

3

Between Pluralist-Acceptance
and Particularist-Refusal

Religious plurality is a description of the fact that there are many religions in the world. But I shall use the term Pluralist-Acceptance here to indicate an hypothesis about plurality in so far as it assumes that Hinduism, Islam, Buddhism, Sikhism and so on exist in 'rough parity'[1] with Christian faith as streams of authentic religious belief and practice. This implies a validity of religious vision which is comparable among the religions, and which therefore calls for an explanation of the whole. For Particularist-Refusers such a project is an impossibility: according to this group the religions speak with such different voices as to render them wholly incomparable. Even the assumption of 'rough parity' must be bogus: there is no bridge, dialogical or otherwise, from one to another. It is small wonder that the debate between representatives of these two types of position has been fierce in recent years.

Before spelling out these positions further I would like to sketch briefly an early version of each, both from the early years of the twentieth century, and this will give a context for the discussion that follows. My first example comes from the German Protestant theologian-sociologist, Ernst Troeltsch (1865–1923), and the second from the High Church Anglican missionary, Charles Freer Andrews (1871–1940), a close friend of and co-worker with Mahatma Gandhi.

In 1901, Ernst Troeltsch published his book *The Absoluteness of Christianity*. It was a study in the eventual superiority of

Christian faith, following a century which had seen the rise of the historical and comparative study of the world's religions. Towards the end of his book Troeltsch wrote:

> Above all, Christianity remains the work of Jesus, having its greatest strength in relation to him and drawing its confidence from the authentic and living guarantee of the grace of God in his personality. Even though we discern the power and activity of God in other heroes and prophets of religion, it is in Christianity, more profoundly than anywhere else, that faith in God is bound up with the vision of the life and passion of him who reveals and guarantees that faith.[2]

The sense of what he called 'personalism' was the deciding factor in the comparison between different religious worldviews. His study of the religions up to 1901 left him convinced that only in Christianity could a real personalized sense of religious humaneness be discerned and this placed Christian faith above other religions. However, by 1923, in a lecture due to be given in Oxford (it was published posthumously – Troeltsch died before giving it), Troeltsch revealed that, as a result of further study, this view was no longer sustainable: there were profound spiritual and humane values present in other religions too. This led Troeltsch to draw the conclusion, startling for its day, that Christianity was one manifestation of divine life alive through one culture: '[Christianity] is God's countenance as revealed to us'; and, more expansively: 'Each of the faiths may experience its contact with the divine life.' Such were the theological conclusions being drawn from investigations in the history of religions, what I have been calling new information from lived religion.

The formulation confining Christianity to its European homelands has, rightly, not found general acceptance among theologians. But the idea that it was no longer appropriate to claim finality for Christ and Christian faith has found general acceptance among Pluralist-Accepters. Between 1901 and 1923 Troeltsch had changed his mind about the value of other religious traditions and allowed the impact of new knowledge its full weight. A line had been crossed.

What now of the other side of the pairing – what I have termed Particularist-Refusal? I take the example of Charles Freer Andrews, not because he is a perfect example of Particularist thinking but because he is a forerunner to the more philosophical and theologically grounded Particularism of the last quarter of the twentieth century.

Charlie Andrews was a Christian missionary who arrived in Delhi in 1904 as a member of the Cambridge Mission to Delhi, inspired by a theology which was broadly speaking Inclusivist. In the same manner as the early Eastern Church Fathers had forged an Inclusivist Christian theological system from the marriage of Greek philosophy and biblical religion, so the Cambridge Mission would seek to do the same but now in the context of Indian thought and practice. As Greek philosophy was 'a providential purpose in the development of Gentile life'[3] prior to the dispensation of the Christian gospel, so Hindu tradition might be a new and different cultural context for the presentation of the Christian message. But Andrews had a gift for developing deep and lasting friendships with Hindus, Muslims, Sikhs and others, and through those friendships new insights about the religions he encountered – not as dry patterns of belief but as living realities for their devotees – brought him to the brink of theological revision. If he was convinced of the eventual superiority of Christian faith in a world of many faiths before his encounter with people of other traditions, then reflections on his encounters moved him towards a different appreciation. Some of the implications of these new friendships and experiences of Indian spiritual life for the Christian approach to other religions are set out in a 'Letter to Gandhi' which is reproduced in the Appendix. The reader should take time to consult this letter before continuing with my analysis of it.

The letter is set in the context of the issue of conversion, which to most Indian religious thinkers offends against the broad inclusivity of Hindu thought and remains a thorny subject in any Christian–Hindu dialogue. Andrews wants to defend the practice of conversion, yet combine it with as much openness and lack of dogmatic spirit as possible. Let me list a number of elements which the letter embodies:

1 Religions are not static systems but dynamic movements. Therefore it should be possible for someone to change religion without coercion.
2 Changing one's religion need not entail rejecting all that was positive and good in what has been left behind.
3 Jesus himself recognized 'faith' in those Gentiles outside the original Jewish Church. Ethnicity did not define or confine true faithfulness.
4 Devotees of whatever tradition have the right of freedom of religion. We should honour 'reverence for all that is good wherever it is found' and at the same time be free to commend our own unique instance of that reverence.
5 The great religions are universal in their intent and this is to be celebrated; therefore we should learn from one another.
6 The religions are not equal in their central structures and purposes and so there should be no mixing up or sliding over of differences between them.
7 Competition between religions for souls should be abandoned, even as we are free to proclaim our own tradition as 'the most complete and inspiring that was ever given to man'.
8 While becoming Christian through baptism does not entail the rejection of that which is good in other religions, baptism's real intent is moral: the renunciation of 'the essential evils of this life'.
9 The motivation in interreligious relationships should be 'to see the best in one another' as 'an essential feature of love'.

There is much in Andrews' presentation to admire, not least the shift from a 'from above' approach to Christian witnessing to one 'from below', which stems from friendships built on respect. Although Andrews was not a systematic theologian as such, it is appropriate to ask whether or not the various elements of his letter cohere as a theological whole. Friendship leads Andrews to admire the 'truth' within another religion but he shies away from the theological task of interpreting how those 'truths' are related to Christian truth as a message with universal intent. At what level do the 'truths' of others make an impact on Christian 'truth'? Is the right of each to proclaim his 'truths' as 'the most complete and inspiring' a function of human rights in the context of modernity only or do those 'truths' have relevance for how Christian faith (or any other faith) has traditionally held its own insights to be superior over others? The giveaway moment in the letter, in my view showing its Achilles heel, is when Andrews couches the purpose of baptism in purely ethical terms, renouncing 'the world, the flesh and the devil'. It is as though signing up for commitment to the way of Christ in baptism, involving the traditional assumption of its theological supremacy over other ways in some objective sense, has been abandoned or at least set on one side.

As time went on, Andrews turned towards a missionary stance which concentrated more on the spiritual or inner world of religious tradition than on the external representations of religious institutional life. Jesus became a figure of non-exclusivistic universal compassion, one with echoes in other traditions and seminal figures. Andrews became slightly less tolerant of theological schemes, even those of his own training, such as the '*logos* doctrine' which imagined other traditions to be paler reflections of the 'incarnate *logos*' embodied most fully in Jesus of Nazareth. Yet he did not abandon this framework entirely, for he later speculated that the compassion of Jesus, the universal 'Son of Man', was also found prior to Jesus in what he called the 'Hindu-Buddhist stream, which . . . had for long ages been the greatest moral and spiritual force in all the world'.[4]

Andrews' encounters with other religions brought him to a new threshold, but he did not take the Pluralist path. He was fearful of 'mixing up' and wanted to maintain a firm hold on differences. But as he took the principal explanation of baptism to be an ethical one he forfeited the decisiveness (uniqueness?) which traditional Christian faith should have warranted. In other words, he refused to enter into debates about the salvific value of other traditions. Hence my claiming him as a prototype Particularist-Refuser.

Let me now turn to the contemporary debate.

Pluralist-Acceptance

The Pluralist approach in the theology of religions sets out an hypothesis which affirms the other major religions as valid and equally salvific paths in relation both to ultimate transcendent reality and to the journey towards mutual critical acceptance of one another. One of the foremost exponents of this view has been the philosopher-theologian John Hick, whose summation of the Pluralist position runs as follows:

> I suggest that the best religious account we can give of the global situation is that of a single ineffable Ultimate Reality whose universal presence is being differently conceived and experienced and responded to within the different human religious traditions.[5]

It is important immediately to add that this view does not entail that all religions are equal in the sense that the different cultural embodiments of religious spirit are merely language and symbolic screens, each suggesting different names for essentially the same transcendent reality. The hypothesis is far more sophisticated than that caricature (which is often heard) suggests. It is likely that the religions are generated by and, in turn, reproduce characteristically different experiences together with the reflexive superstructure of belief and culturally specific formulations. Therefore that which is 'ineffable', by which is meant 'non-reducible to human categories', must of necessity be at least potentially capable of being contemplated in a variety of forms. Pluralism affirms that this is indeed so.

A reasonable picture of the Pluralist-Acceptance option might go like this:

1 Religious identity is mainly inherited as a function of one's birthplace. So: Indonesians are likely to be Muslim; Thais likely to be Buddhist; Europeans likely to be Christian, and so on. This is not a hard and fast observation, for globalization is changing inherited patterns, but even in mixed societies it remains the case, and one which missionary activity or modern immigration patterns have not significantly undermined.

2 Religions are outworkings of the religious experience that resides at the heart of tradition. Christianity exists as a vehicle for reproducing or re-enacting in many cultural forms the core experience of knowing God as 'boundless love', stemming initially from Jesus of Nazareth and the response to him. The rationality of this ever-changing tradition is born of trusting this experience, a trust which has 'proved' itself over a long period. The same will be true of other world traditions and it is this which brings them into 'rough parity'.

3 The notion of God's 'boundless love' leads Christians to expect to see the effects of God's presence and activity in many places in the world. The fruits of religious practice, in terms of the transformative potential of religious experience in raising human beings to relationship with that spiritual reality which transcends the

> The notion of God's 'boundless love' leads Christians to expect to see the effects of God's presence and activity in many places in the world

world and which Westerners know as 'God', confirm this across the world religions.

4   The distinction between the ultimate 'unknowability' and the human 'knowability' of transcendent spirit – a distinction which arises because of the finitude of the human mind and the infinity of (transcategorial) ultimate reality – is present within all traditions. We do not know God in Godself, but only as a mediated reality, and this is the case whether or not we are talking of theistic or non-theistic, prophetic or mystical, dualist or unitive traditions.

5   Differences in theology and philosophy derive from characteristic different experiences and explorations of their meanings in terms of varied systems of cultural thought, art and cultic expression, these explorations being the subject matter of any course in the study of religion. This mediated sense of our human awareness, our experience of ultimate reality, is the ground for thinking of the different religions as different orientations of culturally conditioned human responses to the same infinite transcendent reality.

6   Not all beliefs and practices of the religions are acceptable. Deciding between good and bad, true and false religions is now a matter of cross-cultural and cross-religious dialogue, as well as engaging with critical thinking in the light of what we know of the world through knowledge which is gained from many disciplines. (So-called religious fundamentalism, for example, would not be acceptable on this reckoning, as it refuses to engage with any kind of critical thinking.)

7   In dialogue religions should be open to being changed, as a result of receiving insights from others, through a process of integration and transformation.[6]

In dialogue religions should be open to being changed, as a result of receiving insights from others, through a process of integration and transformation

On the whole, pluralists will expect to discover 'complementarities' between traditions as a means of bringing different religious experiences and conceptualities into relationship.

Attempts have been made to portray the Pluralist option on the basis of analogy, two of the most popular images being the parable of 'the blind men and the elephant' and the image of 'many roads up the same mountain'. On the first analogy, the story has it that an elephant is brought before a group of blind men and they each touch a different part of its bulky physique. One touches a leg and reports that the elephant is a pillar, another the trunk and says it is a great snake, and so on. The analogy is not that the men experience different parts of the elephant (standing for ultimate reality) but that each experiences the whole of the elephant from his own partial standpoint. However, the criticism is often made that the analogy breaks down as a parable for Pluralist-Acceptance, for it relies on someone knowing that the blind men are in fact touching the same elephant and there can be no such person available if the parable is applied analogously to the religions. There can be no confirmation that each is touching the elephant if there is no agent external to the scene, and the absence of an external agent reflects what is the case in real life.

The image of many roads up the same mountain – the roads representing the religions and the mountain-top being our encounter with ultimate reality – is also in common use. This seems to me to be even less satisfactory, as Pluralist-Acceptance does not imagine that each tradition shares the same nameable mountain summit. If the mountain-top extended into heavenly clouds and remained hidden from view then perhaps it would have some limited traction as an image.

A third image from the theologian Rosemary Ruether comes closer to the spirit of what the Pluralist hypothesis intends:

Although there is much overlap among religions, they also represent a broad spectrum of possible ways of experiencing the divine.
Some may focus on the historical struggle for justice, some on
the renewal of natural processes, and some on mystical ecstasy.
Each has incarnated its way of symbolizing life and its relationship to the higher powers in unique ways that make it impossible
simply to translate one religion to the other, or to create some
abstraction of them all into a universal, ethical faith . . .[7]

She continues as though each tradition views the whole of
reality through limited framed windows:

True universality lies in accepting one's own finiteness, one's own
particularity and, in so doing, not making that particularity the
only true faith, but allowing other particularities to stand side by
side with yours as having equal integrity. Each is limited and particular and yet each is, in its own way, an adequate way of experiencing the whole for a particular people at a particular time.[8]

Through their particular windows each views the whole, yet each
is limited by the frame of the window itself. It is as though each
tradition can never fully reflect all that needs to be said about
the human relationship with transcendent ultimate reality. In one
tradition justice is the uppermost concern, in another intimacy
with the earth, in another a sense of mystical unity, and so on.

Ruether's picture brings out the complementarities between
traditions, emphasizing how dominant insights have marked
different religious traditions and how no one tradition has been
capable of highlighting all insights adequately in one outlook.
If the critique is made that the analogy still requires one person
to have a 'windowless' point of view in order for us to know
that the different views are complementary, then in defence
of the analogy all that one can say is that it does not pretend
to objective knowledge; rather, the complementarity is arrived
at inductively, from the various perspectives of partial insight

each grounded in distinctive experiences. Pluralist-Acceptance remains an hypothesis striving to make sense of the different perspectives offered by the different religions.

Particularist-Refusal

There are perhaps two broad objections to this whole way of framing the discussion of theology of religions and I want to consider each of these in turn. However, as these critiques have been part and parcel of a developing stance now often called particularity[9] (which I am naming Particularist-Refusal), I will therefore consider them under that heading. But, as with Pluralist-Acceptance, let me first set out this position in the form of a series of propositions:

1 Each religion is *sui generis*, and therefore what we call the 'religions' are, strictly speaking, incapable of being compared one with another; no common core exists.
2 Religious experience is constrained and shaped by language, culture and history, and therefore there is no such thing as the 'pure essence' of religious experience.
3 It is only possible to speak from a specific point of view, i.e. from within a tradition, for there cannot be a viewpoint equidistant from all traditions by which any one tradition can be judged.
4 The classical period of Christian history, especially as embodied in the doctrine of the incarnation of Christ and the Holy Trinity, represents true Christian identity and therefore the point from which other religions are to be judged.
5 No salvific potency resides in other traditions, though they may be involved in God's hope for humanity and therefore the spirit of God may be working through them to inspire individuals who live within them, even as we have no way of knowing this.

Let the following citation from the Catholic theologian Joseph DiNoia provide a working summary of this position:

> ... other religions are to be valued by Christians, not because they are channels of grace or means of salvation for their adherents, but because they play a real but as yet not fully specifiable role in the divine plan to which the Christian community bears witness.[10]

From a traditional Christian perspective, on this view, other religions cannot be thought to be vehicles of salvation because salvation is a Christian term and other traditions have different terminologies and conceptualities which cannot be equated with Christian salvation. This need not entail, however, that other religions are valueless; rather, simply that we are not in a position to know how other religions correspond to God's hope for the world. It may seem that this is a form of decent agnosticism, a not-knowing if or how other religions are to be valued given the evident incommensurability between them. Yet closer inspection shows it to be a form of refusal, that is, a turning away from the question of theology of religions altogether.

Other writers, called Comparative theologians and discussed more fully in the next chapter, have spoken openly in a similar vein. For example, James Fredericks writes: 'Although abandoning attempts to erect a systematic theology of religions may be difficult for Christian theologians to accept, honesty to our current situation requires this of us.'[11] The suggestion is that we are not yet in a position to know the meaning of plurality until we have learned from a longer period of dialogue between religions. Best call a moratorium on theology of religions! For this reason, it seems to me that Particularist-Refusal really is not a form of theology of religions, for it does not present itself in this way – in fact, quite the opposite!

It is worth exploring the Particularist-Refusal view further in relation to its critique of Pluralism, thereby in the process drawing out the contours of both positions more sharply. First, the complaint is often heard that Pluralist views assume a common core experience of salvation among the religions, which turns out to be Christian salvation. The objection is that it is not possible to tell whether or not another tradition is salvific, for criteria to this effect are not available outside the Christian tradition itself. 'Salvation' is a Christian category and ought not to be conflated with the cognates from other traditions, such as nirvana (Buddhism) or liberation from *moksa* (Hinduism). What is incumbent on the Christian theologian, for these objectors, is to lay out the principles by which salvation is offered to the world, as this has been declared and honed in Christian faith, and then investigate the implications of these for religious plurality. So, if we summarize the Christian gospel as the witness that God has drawn near to the world in the person of Jesus Christ who is 'the particular historical pattern on this planet of God's universal action to liberate intelligent beings from anger, greed, and ignorance and unite them to the divine life of wisdom, compassion, and love',[12] the question 'How then do we respond to religious plurality?' arises secondarily. The gospel vision is universalist in the sense that the divine love is offered to all peoples and cultures, and there is no reason to imagine that this love is confined to the Christian expression of it. Therefore, to this extent, it may be glimpsed from within another religious path even if it is not named as Christian. Moreover, while this view accepts that there may be truths which are expressed more sharply in other traditions than in Christianity and from which Christians can learn, it refuses to entertain a Pluralist outlook. It does not necessarily expect everyone to become Christian but it does hold to the confession that salvation is by Christ alone, for this is a given *sine qua non* of Christian faith.

Is this expansive Christian vision a real objection to Pluralist-Acceptance? The answer must be 'Yes', for it assumes that Christ alone is the unique saviour. But in another sense it is hardly an objection for it does not address the issue of the religions as such as vehicles or contexts of independent transcendent value. It remains focused on individuals in other traditions. In one sense it seems little advance on the 1990 San Antonio conference of the World Council of Churches (WCC) which affirmed: 'We cannot point to any other way of salvation than Jesus Christ; at the same time we cannot set limits to the saving power of God.'[13]

This objection to Pluralism, it seems to me, is less of an objection than an evasion of theology of religions. It is best envisaged as a 'witness stance': the love of God is all-embracing and potent for the entire world, but it refuses to make judgements about other traditions as ways of saving faith. The fact of the sole reliance on Christ as the cause or completion of the salvation, which is being everywhere sought or enacted, in reality draws it into either an Exclusivist or Inclusivist category. It does this in spite of the fact that Particularists object to those categories.

That was a soft objection. A more hardened objection, which I have already hinted at above, has emerged from those who have absorbed the work of George Lindbeck in his influential book *The Nature of Doctrine*,[14] and especially when this is combined with the philosophy of Wittgenstein. Basically, the complaint is that the whole theology of religious endeavour is based on a mistake, the mistake being that the religions are so different in their fundamental orientations, each being shaped in highly specific and particular ways, that it is worthless speculating on the salvific validity of other traditions. The formal term for this supposed state of affairs is 'incommensurability'. Even when it looks as though

> Basically, the complaint is that the whole theology of religious endeavour is based on a mistake

there may be a great deal of resonance across the high fences of traditions they remain incommensurable. As Lindbeck says, using the example of love:

> The datum that all religions recommend something which can be called 'love' towards that which is taken to be most important ('God') is a banality as uninteresting as the fact that all languages are (or were) spoken. The significant things are the distinctive patterns of story, belief, ritual, and behaviours that give 'love' and 'God' their specific and sometimes contradictory meanings.[15]

For this type of response it is language, tradition and concept which are primary for religions: followers do not codify the 'same religious experience' in the different symbolic languages represented by the historical religions, but the interpretative framework precedes the experience and shapes it according to complex contextual streamlined constructions. In other words, language, tradition and concept cohere in related ways internally to a religion. Religions should be approached as 'wholes': it would be mistaken to imagine that a word which appears across traditions, for example 'justice', entails a single sense of meaning across those traditions.

One prominent voice who has taken this line of enquiry with due seriousness is the Catholic theologian Gavin D'Costa. For D'Costa the only viable approach to the religions is from what he terms a 'tradition-specific' point of view. This entails that we make no immediate judgement about other traditions as such, though it is possible that followers of other traditions may be animated by the Spirit of God, for it is God's declared intention, according to Christian Scripture, that all should be saved and know God. As a Catholic, D'Costa subscribes to what he perceives as a continuous stream of Christian orthodoxy which is capable of being open towards people of other traditions in dialogue and cooperation, and might even stand to learn from others, though it will be learning which both 'fulfils' others and which enables Christian faith to expand its own horizons in different cultural directions. D'Costa's own summary reads as follows:

> Christ is the cause of all salvation and the Church is Christ's body on earth, the means by which all grace is mediated. How this grace might be mediated to those outside the Church is an area that is not defined or resolved, but that this grace is mediated to those outside the Church is a certainty.[16]

It is interesting that one can have certainty about something we know nothing about!

Taking that sense of certainty to heart, most Catholic theologians, especially in the mould of Vatican II, have been less hesitant than D'Costa in affirming the role of the religions as such as vehicles of transcendent grace, precisely because that grace requires historical and embodied mediation for effectiveness. D'Costa himself used to subscribe to this understanding[17] but under the impact of postmodern influences promoting 'incommensurability' he cannot but limit the possibility of the presence of grace to individual human hearts, though other religions might remain, in a traditional fashion, preparations for the gospel. Christ is the origin of all salvation.

In recent years the critique of Pluralist theologies of religions which relies on postmodern assumptions has been extensive. However, many of these critiques have been answered in various publications.[18] Let me now offer three responses to the critiques by way of illustration.

First, some critiques are made on the basis of misperception. For example, it is not the case that Pluralism assumes that all religions are simply different symbolic expressions of the same putative religious experience at the core of each tradition. John Hick, for example, has been very clear that the organizing categories of the mind play a significant role in both the reception and shaping of religious experience itself. Our experiencing is always 'experiencing-as' – Hindus undergo characteristically Hindu experience, Christians characteristically Christian experience, and so on. The religions are responses to the same ultimate reality but from within differently developed cultures. Christian love may not be the same as Buddhist compassion, but that does not mean that they are therefore as incommensurable as postmoderns suppose. In practical terms, of course, Christian love and Buddhist compassion might amount to the same thing: the relief of unnecessary suffering; the critique of oppressive structures around the world; the promotion of interdependent living. But the point is that Pluralist-Acceptance has never assumed that all religions are effectively the same 'underneath'. In fact, Pluralist-Acceptance was developed as a way of seeking to honour the differences while according value to the 'rough parity' between them.

Second, the association of Pluralist views with Enlightenment 'universal reason', which has fallen under suspicion in postmodernist times, is also a mischievous caricature. In so far as Enlightenment rationality functions to exclude even notions of 'revelation' then the theological suspicion is deserved. However, 'revelation' should not be used to trump rationality as though all canons of reason should be sacrificed at its altar. 'Revelation' is glimpsed through the religious experience of transcendent reality, which in turn is configured differently according to language, tradition and culture. It is this recognition of real 'revelation' being responded to through a diversity of religious experiences that calls for interpretation. The observation about differences between traditions, because of the way in which traditions are perceived to have developed contextually over time, simply presents a new challenge for theologians and others and one which cannot be bypassed by retreating into a bunker called 'tradition'. Besides, 'tradition' itself is far from being a settled or easy concept, for which parts or periods of tradition should we count as our reference point for determining Christian identity? As suggested earlier, Particularist-Refusal relies on the classical period of the Church Fathers as the period yielding what has been called the 'grammar of tradition'.

But it is no accident that advocates of a 'tradition-specific' approach can often seem to assume a rather uncritical approach to belief and faith at this point. It is by no means obvious why the classical period should be the defining reference point for Christian identity for all time. As Harry Kuitert has written of classical christology:

> God-on-earth is first of all an interpretation, a view which people attributed to the Jesus of the Gospels in a particular time and culture, a phase in reception history, albeit one which lasted a long time and left deep traces. Nevertheless, it is a phase.[19]

That might seem an unsettling conclusion to draw, but it is not unreasonable if we take the full impact of critical historical con- sciousness to heart. 'Tradition', it seems, is a fluid category, and this can be demonstrated historically. So, since the early days, beginning even in the New Testament, Christian faith has adapted to new environments, absorbed new influences and modified its forms. Sometimes this has happened in relation to other religions or religious philosophies – as, for example, in the shift from a Hebrew context to a largely Greek philosophical framework in the first centuries, or when a twentieth-century figure such as Bede Griffiths adopts a Hindu Vedanta matrix for Christian thought[20] – and sometimes through interaction with secular (for want of a better term) insights – as, for example, in the wholesale reshaping of Christianity under the influences of mod- ernity. It has even led some to adopt a spirituality of so-called dual identity.[21] Locating Christianity in the classical period alone is too essentialist a strategy. The future also has a claim.

Third, maximizing the implications of the postmodern stress on the role of language and culture in shaping experience, as does Lindbeck, need not of itself, as I have said, automatically drive religious traditions into a position of incommensurability. But there are other assumptions at work in the stress on incommensurability and, in the case of Lindbeck, these derive from his Lutheran background. Marianne Moyaert comprehensively and brilliantly lists these in a series of contrasts: (a) the world is a place of chaos where nature and grace are pitted against one another; (b) the church exists to foster Christian identity in a sphere apart from the world; (c) human beings are dominated by the effects of sin and therefore exist only in need of redemption through Christ and the biblical word which presents Christ.[22] It can easily be seen how a cultural-linguistic view of religious tradition dovetails easily with these classical Lutheran assumptions. The Catholic philosophical theologian, David Tracey, observes this nicely:

> Lindbeck's substantive theological position is a methodologic-
> ally sophisticated version of Barthian confessionalism. The hands
> may be the hands of Wittgenstein and Geertz but the voice is
> the voice of Karl Barth.[23]

In other words, the analysis of how religious experience is embodied and developed through language, culture and practical life is made to serve an agenda which thinks of the world as a locus of God's absence rather than presence and of the Church as a self-referential confessing community rather than a sacramental pilgrim community in dialogue with the world. Over against this whole approach I have emphasized that such a model of religious understanding need not be hijacked by an outlook which promotes incommensurability over resonance.

Summary

Religions which aim to transform the world in order that the world may be conformed to a vision of fulfilled humanity, just and peaceful relationships and a purpose which is centred in transcendent awareness nurture believers in matrices which are essentially earthen vessels, to borrow language from St Paul. Theology needs to make sense of the information that comes from encounters, friendships and accurate knowledge of what the traditions stand for. My contention is that the Christian sense of the boundlessness of the love of God expects there to be salvation at work throughout the world universally, albeit inevitably involving distortions and varying degrees. Interpreting the genuine spirituality that comes through the lives, scriptures and histories of others relies not only on the reasoning associated with tradition but also on responsiveness to new information. Sometimes new information breaks the mould of what has been valued in the past – as has happened to Christian faith in the light of new information from science or from the rise of critical historical and philosophical thinking. Taking both of these contemporary realities seriously seems to me to call for an approach that goes beyond the traditional assumption of Christian faith's theological finality and therefore superiority. In this sense, Pluralist-Acceptance models respond to our new awareness more satisfyingly than those which assume Christianity's absoluteness prior to any encounter with people who have been nurtured in other spiritual ways.

Earlier I noted that the German Christian sociologist, historian and theologian, Ernst Troeltsch, changed his mind between 1901 and 1923, after further study and recognition of

> The Christian sense of the boundlessness of the love of God expects there to be salvation at work throughout the world universally

the 'personalism' also at work within other religions. Emphasizing historical contextualization this brought him to the brink of Pluralist-Acceptance. It was not until the end of the century that other Christian theologians began to have similar inklings of the need for change. In between stands a missionary with a generous heart and an open creativity, Charles Freer Andrews. Andrews more or less outgrew his constraining Inclusivist *logos* theology in the light of encounters and friendships yet could not quite allow himself to entertain a Pluralist outlook. This placed him in what I might call a proto-Particularist category. But this shies away from a theology of religions proper, as his Letter to Gandhi demonstrates. In this sense Particularist-Refusal is born of a kind of anxiety which knows that the Exclusivist–Inclusivist dynamic is insufficient in the face of new data, yet cannot entertain the thought of having to surrender Christian absolutism. Pluralist-Acceptance is prepared to take that step as the next step in an evolving life of faithfulness.

4

Between Christian mission and interfaith dialogue

Two stirrings

Something was stirring in the decades before and after the turn of the twentieth century. In 1893 the World Parliament of Religions was convened in Chicago on the occasion of the great Columbian Exposition (1892–3), celebrating America's techno-logical achievements 500 years after the arrival of Christopher Columbus in the New World. It was, commented Richard Hughes Seager, 'a triumphalistic celebration of the conquest of the continent, and an announcement of America's economic and political ambitions overseas'.[1] But triumphalism was not the only factor at work. A group of American liberal Christians organized a multireligious platform for discussing the ethical and theological issues arising from the exhibition itself and for uniting a common religious front against perceived irreligious and impersonal forces.[2] The star of the occasion was undoub-tedly the Hindu reformist, Swami Vivekananda, who had travelled from India. Here is a well-known paragraph from his opening speech to the Parliament:

> Sectarianism, bigotry, and its horrible descendant, fanaticism, have long possessed this beautiful earth. They have filled the earth with violence, drenched it often and often with human blood, destroyed civilization, and sent whole nations to despair. Had it not been for these horrible demons, human society would be far more advanced than it is now . . . I fervently hope that the

bell that tolled this morning in honour of this convention may be the death-knell of fanaticism, of all persecutions with the sword or with the pen, and of all uncharitable feelings between persons wending their way to the same goal.[3]

In this passage, Vivekananda speaks eloquently about the role that religious fault-lines have played in fomenting violence around the world and how a dialogical future is needed if peace is to reign in the world. The current enthusiastic promotion of dialogue between religions by Western governments, during the post-September 11 first decade of the twenty-first century, echoes Vivekananda's main motive for interfaith dialogue. But we should note also his theological assumption – born of his Indian Hindu ethos – that 'religions are wending their way to the same goal'. This was and remains of course a contentious issue in the theological interpretation of religious plurality. However, for Vivekananda, it did not mean the religions should merge into one religion:

The Christian is not to become a Hindu or a Buddhist, nor a Hindu or a Buddhist to become a Christian. But each must assimilate the spirit of the others and yet preserve his individuality and grow according to his own law of growth.[4]

In his speeches, Vivekananda brings into the open two assumptions which have shaped the dialogue movement ever since: (i) the integrity of the religions is to be preserved, and (ii) growth in religious identity will, from now on, involve interaction with and through 'the spirit of the others'.

Then in 1910 another global gathering was convened, this time in Edinburgh, for Christian missionaries from around the world, under the banner 'the evangelization of the world in this generation'. This convention was summoned in order that mission practitioners from different Christian denominations might share reflections in the light of experiences which, in turn, might shape Christian world outreach accordingly. But practitioners reported variously and many spoke of expectations which were subverted by what they encountered abroad. 'Heathen lands afar' (as the old missionary hymn had it) were not necessarily so heathen and many missionaries reported high philosophy, impressive spirituality and humane ethics elsewhere. This left a question mark over theologies which assumed an absence of sacred presence in other cultures and civilizations. Consider the following example from Commission 4 of the Edinburgh Conference reports:

> Yet when all is said, there is a deep truth in the Hindu conviction of the nothingness of the world in comparison with God. If we must choose, it is better to believe that God is all and the world nothing, than to believe that the world is all and God nothing, which is a view widely prevailing today in Christian lands. No Christian holds this latter view either in theory or in practice. Yet have not both our Christian theology and practice become deeply tinged with the prevailing naturalism of the West?[5]

Following critical remarks on the caste system and Hinduism's lack of engagement with other social questions, acknowledgement is here given to the challenge which the Hindu worldview of 'union with the All' presents to Christian faith. Furthermore, this citation also brings out the secular context, a kind of third dialogue partner, within which encounter happens. Clearly, new information from encounter and experience was inviting deeper reflection on the nature of Christian mission and, by implication, of assumed Christian finality. Already by 1910, the chairman of the commission, David Cairns, included the judgement that in their 'nobler elements' other religions showed evidence of 'the working of the Spirit of God'.[6]

A basic tension

I cite these examples at the turn of the twentieth century in order to underline that that century was heir to a perceived tension between Christian mission and interfaith dialogue. As will become clear, that tension remains with us, in spite of theological efforts to dampen its severity. On the one hand, there is the absoluteness animating Christian missions, and, on the other hand, there is the assumed parity behind the movement for dialogue. Sharpening the tension, one could say that Mission involves telling, giving, and bestowing from a superior to an inferior, while Dialogue equals listening, receiving, and sharing among equals.

But is this a real or imaginary problem? For some, it is imaginary because the polarization involves a caricature of both concepts. First, in respect of Mission: if we disentangle Mission's past alignment from colonialist power and imperialist aggression then we dissolve the caricature of Mission. If the meaning of Mission is conceived now simply as the conveying of a religion's core experience by narrating its fundamental story – being a witness – surely that would present no ethical obstacles to dialogue with other faiths? Second, in respect of Dialogue: remove the caricature assumption that all religions are the same underneath their cultural veneers of language and intellectual histories and Dialogue can reclaim its proper meaning as 'reasoning across worlds'. The claim is that by so exorcising the caricatures Mission and Dialogue can coexist, each with its integrity in the changing picture of overall Christian understanding. Moreover, whatever friction remains between them could even be turned to theological advantage. Deprived of power, missioners can learn appreciation for other religions and that opens the door to dialogue. In turn, dialoguers ought to thrive on differences and disagreements and this requires respect for the missionary thrust of religions as the conveyance of religious experience and belief through the rehearsing of different narratives.

In part, the easing of the tension between Mission and Dialogue has been helped by developments on both sides of the divide: both concepts have acquired a multi-dimensional sense. So Mission is not now simply church extension or the 'saving of souls', plucking individuals from a blighted world. Christian Mission is defined as participation in the *Missio Dei*: the mission of God in and to the world, and in which the Church participates but does not control or circumscribe. The *Missio Dei* encompasses an expanded portfolio of scenarios and activities: evangelism/witness (giving account of the hope within us); inculturation (translating the message into cultur- ally relevant terms, in different languages and contexts); world development and nation-building (through commitment to justice, peace and the sustainability of creation); and, finally, dialogue between religions and ideologies (in the search for greater understanding between peoples and communities and a deeper grasp on reality). The gradual shift in the definition of Mission through the twentieth century is neatly captured if we compare Edinburgh's 1910 conference – 'the evangelization of the world in this generation' – with the proposal at the 1993 WCC conference in Canberra, which proposed the widest perspective possible by announcing that 'a reconciled and renewed creation is the goal of the churches' mission'. This is a universalizing radical shift in understanding indeed!

Alongside these expansions in missiology through the twentieth century, other developments and changing assumptions in the theological world helped to defuse missionary anxiety about dialogue. These included:

1 recognition that the notion of 'revelation-cum-salvation' runs through the religions and not between Christianity and the

others. While there may be a distinction between 'revelation' and 'salvation' there must be no separation;

2 greater reliance on the universal thrust of the Christian understanding of God as boundless love – with the implication that love is not the sole possession of Christianity, a factor which can be verified in other traditions;

3 positive acceptance of the continuing place of other religions in God's purposes and not simply as facts to be noted in history. A WCC meeting of Catholic, Protestant and Orthodox theologians in 1991 affirmed that other religions represent both a *searching* for God and a *finding* of God.[7] This was considered quite a breakthrough just 12 years after the acceptance of the WCC's *Guidelines for Dialogue*.

It is easy to see how these developments not only rendered Mission less theologically confrontational but also added to the theological permission for dialogue as such.

What now of any parallel developmental vein in relation to interfaith dialogue? This has come to involve more than the theological exchange of fixed positions. Classically, now, dialogue has similarly evolved as a multi-dimensional concern, with the following elements: theological dialogue (of the head) concerned with understanding the presence of God beyond Christian categories alone; practical dialogue (of the hands) whereby communities cooperate across boundaries of difference for the sake of the shared common good between peoples; spiritual dialogue (of the heart) involving learning from the experience of ultimate reality as this is reflected in different traditions; and, finally, the dialogue of life (of basic humanity) which embraces a shared sense of facing the trials and joys of life among neighbours and citizens, as a matter of existential living. Writers and activists involved in dialogical work have evolved a version of 'rules for encounter', most of which turn on the values of respect, listening, openness to learn, and self-criticism.

Authentic dialogue is not a form of conflict resolution (although it may place the roots of historical conflicts in better perspective and thereby may lead to some healing of memories), but is essentially a *religious* encounter. The expectation that dialoguers learn from one other seems tantamount to a form of relationship which is defined by mutual accountability.

If, alongside a changing view of missiology, shifts in theological patterns added momentum to a whole process, have there been comparable developments on the Dialogue side? I believe there have been and they are essentially concerned with deepening the impact of critical thinking as an intrinsic component of the dialogical endeavour. At its root, Dialogue as a framework for seeking religious truth assumes that no one tradition can possibly have the whole grasp of what is ultimate (in theistic terms, 'God'). The dialogical theologian, Leonard Swidler, has put this succinctly in relation to our knowing more generally:

> Our understanding of truth statements, in short, has become 'deabsolutized' – it has become 'relational'; that is, all statements about reality are now seen to be related to the historical context, praxis, intentionality, perspective, etc, of the speaker, and in that sense no longer 'absolute,' unlimited.[8]

If this is the case in relation to our human knowing across many fields of critical enquiry then surely it will apply with even greater force when it comes to theological knowing. For there is an added complication in the theological field, in so far as the object of our knowing is referred to as 'transcendent reality'. In religion, our knowing is bound to be even more indirect.

Of course at one level this kind of observation is wholly traditional, for God is beyond the mind. There is always 'more' to ultimate reality than can be captured in experience or ritual or verbal formulae. But this shift towards 'interpretative perspective' deepens the radical sense of linguistic inadequacy or limited viewing, summarized in the affirmation of truth as 'deabsolutized'. If we accept with full seriousness the implications of this shift, it leads us to the assessment of Rabbi Irving Greenberg that 'there has to be a plurality of legitimate symbols if the divine intention is to raise humans to the fullest capacities of life.'[9] Similarly, the dialogical theologian, Paul Mojzes, has included the following in his 'rules for dialogue': 'Soul-searching and mutual enrichment should be part of the dialogue. Neither truth is absolute. Each partner needs the other in order to get a more complete picture of truth.'[10] In other words, interfaith dialogue has been creating a climate that supersedes the original theological permission for it that we gave ourselves a generation ago. Dialogue is more than a process and becomes the framework for exploring religious truth itself across boundaries. Dialogue can be a processive 'passing over' and returning enlarged and enriched, but it can also be more than a process of exchange: an orientation on transcendent reality which exceeds all manifestations, and involving what Jain tradition thinks of as 'non-onesidedness' (*anekantvad*). If we live in a deabsolutized world, then Dialogue is not just learning *about*, or *with*, but also *through* one another.

> There is always 'more' to ultimate reality than can be captured in experience or ritual or verbal formulae

> There has to be a plurality of legitimate symbols if the divine intention is to raise humans to the fullest capacities of life

The problem continued

I began this chapter by outlining a tension between the two concepts of Mission and Dialogue, and then showing how the stand-off between the two needs to be seen in a more nuanced fashion than a simple interpretation of both concepts at first allows. Nevertheless I believe that there is more of a problem embedded in the relationship between Mission and Dialogue than either a simple clean-up operation about dispelling conceptual caricatures or an expanding of terms might lead us to think.

The problem can be illustrated with reference to the papal encyclical, *Redemptoris Missio* (1990), which avers, on the one hand, that 'Dialogue does not originate from tactical concerns or self-interest, but is an activity with its own guiding principles, requirements and dignity' and that 'Those engaged in this dialogue must be consistent with their own religious traditions and convictions, and be open to understanding those of the other party without pretense or close-mindedness, but with truth, humility and frankness, knowing that dialogue can enrich each side.'[11] This appears to be permission *par excellence* for dialogue without strings. But what is given with one hand is again taken back by the other: 'Dialogue should be conducted and implemented with the conviction that *the church is the ordinary means of salvation* and that *she alone* possesses the fullness of the means of salvation.'[12] In other words, Dialogue remains subordinate to the traditional Mission stance of the Church. Sure, it is not the old Mission as saving the *massa damnata*, but it is Mission as a result of the superiority of the Church as God's chosen instrument of salvation.

Something similar was reflected in the document *Dominus Iesus* (2000), which spoke of other religions as being 'in a gravely deficient situation in comparison with those who, in the Church, have the fullness of the means of salvation'.[13] The consequences of this stance were alluded to in a letter sent by the Pope to the Italian Senator, Marcello Pera, agreeing that 'an interreligious dialogue in the strict sense of the term is not possible',[14] the reason being that dialogue would involve placing the final truth of Christian conviction in parenthesis. Instead, interfaith dialogue should be limited to ethical collaboration in dealing with the needs of society.

This example is from the Catholic world, but similar sentiments could be illustrated from the Protestant and Orthodox worlds. It seems that questioning the finality of Christian faith is not an option, even from the point of view of the expanded *Missio Dei*.

Mediator: theology of religions

I hope we can see now how Mission and Dialogue represent two approaches to interfaith relations, each carrying different expectations and assumptions, but remaining uneasy bedfellows. Therefore, still we ask: is it possible to square the circle between Mission and Dialogue satisfactorily? I suggest that if Mission and Dialogue are to communicate with one another they require a mediator and that is supplied by the theology of religions. This mediatorial role can be depicted diagrammatically, as shown in Figure 1.

Since at least the 1960s there have been revisions at both of the conceptual ends of the troubled relationship between

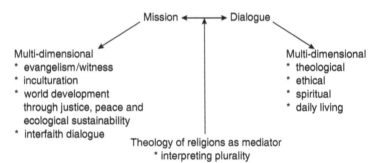

Figure 1 Theology of religions as a mediator between Mission and Dialogue

Mission and Dialogue and these changes are propelling each side towards the other. My thesis is that, as these changes take effect, the need for a theology of religions which can interpret one side to the other grows stronger. From a Mission perspective the task of theology is to clarify the basic Christian experience in the light of changing knowledge and contextual awareness, including our multifaith awareness. From the Dialogue perspective, the task of theology is to articulate the authenticity of difference between the religions together with their belongingness to one another as part of a greater notion of truth. The theology of religions draws these perspectives into relationship.

I am proposing that the theology of religions seeks to interpret the meaning of religious plurality in the light of what we know of other traditions, our experience of their impact in dialogue and practice (their goodness and their negative effects), and the role of critical reasoning (the recognition of history and culture in formulating religious beliefs, spiritualities, ethical postures, and so on). It notes that a religious account of transcendent vision and human transformation is glimpsed through a particular concrete focus, which may be a scripture, a person/founder, or simply our human placing as part of the natural world. In other words, the religions are rooted in concrete experience (particular) but are expansive in their intention and effects (universal). This dynamic is a source both of glory and anxiety – glory in that the experience of ultimate reality that has been glimpsed through a particular means cannot be confined to its originating locus, and it thus inspires missionary activity or, structurally at least, a universalist-minded theology; but also anxiety in that if there are others who similarly glimpse ultimate reality and yet are phenomenologically very different from oneself, then the discomforting question 'what is "God" (to speak theistically) up to?' arises, accompanied often by a sense of existential alarm. Such differences may be not only a source of anxiety but also of suspicion and, as we know all too often, even conflict.

The theology of religions interprets this structure of particularity and universal relevance among the religions in different ways. Here are three possibilities, which correspond to the approaches outlined in Chapters 2 and 3 of this book:

1 It is possible to project one's own particular experience and hold that the universal applicability of the truth which it glimpses, and which is codified in tradition (and its disputes), ought to be the only path for anyone and everyone to follow. In other words, the universality must be defined by the particularity of your own glimpsing: everyone should become Christian, with the consequence that Mission entails the transfer of people from all other traditions into the Christian Church. This is the Exclusivist-Repudiation position.

2 It is possible to project one's own particular experience and hold that the universal applicability of the truth which it glimpses, and which is codified in tradition (and its disputes), ought to lead us to expect to discover other experiences of good and noble worth. On this view, the theology constrains us to hold that other kinds of particularity are necessarily measured by the experience of one's own tradition. In Christian terms, this is done by saying that what is manifest in Jesus is either the origin or the goal, or both, of the universal presence of transcendent reality immanent in the world. It entails that the fullness of religious vision lies with the Christian version of it, but others might participate in that fullness in differing degrees and according to their different histories and cultural development. Mission exists for the purposes of alerting others to the real truth of the Spirit at work within them. This is the Inclusivist-Toleration position.

3 It is possible to project one's own particular experience and hold that the universal applicability of the truth which it glimpses, and which is codified in tradition (and its disputes), is necessary for the world and its transformation, but necessary in company with other histories which have also exhibited vitality and transformative power. Each religion has a view of the whole of reality through the window of its particular glimpsing but it is a partial viewing. Mission entails offering revelatory insight but now in relationships of critical mutual regard. This is the Pluralist-Acceptance position.

We ask now: how do these three positions relate to the tension between Mission and Dialogue? All three positions here accept a role for Mission; that is, all three accept that there is a Christian story to relate and that others should hear it, whether that's for conversion, or for their edification that something greater is available than what they have known thus far, or for the sake of sharing and learning from the differences. But how do they deal with the new information from Dialogue?

Approach (1) has obvious difficulties. If your missiology leads you to expect benightedness (at worst) or a vague, diffuse or misdirected (at best) spirituality elsewhere then you are prob-ably embroiled in a serious misrepresentation of others. So for example, the Protestant Hendrik Kraemer, one of the chief architects in the theory of discontinuity between Christianity and other religions, once wrote:

> Islam in its constitutive elements and apprehensions must be called a superficial religion. The grand simplicity of its concep-tion of God cannot efface this fact and retrieve its patent super-ficiality in regard to the most essential problems of religious life. Islam might be called a religion that has almost no questions and no answers.[15]

From a Dialogue perspective, this is an astonishing statement from a scholar of Islam! It is no wonder that many Muslims (and others) have wondered about the validity of the dialogical invitation from Christian quarters. Where is the mutual respect? Where is the wrestling with Islam as Muslim interpreters see their tradition and not as Christian outsiders look upon it?

The most common position in Christian circles is approach (2). God, according to the expanded idea of the *Missio Dei*, is everywhere but our glimpsing of God can only be measured by the Christian conceptual framework. From the Dialogue angle the difficulties with this are well known. How can Jesus initiate the salvation of the Buddhist or the Hindu, both of whom belong to traditions that are older than the appearance of Jesus on earth? What does it mean, conceptually, for the incarnate Word or the resurrected Christ or the Spirit of God – choose your Christian formulation of words – to be operative in the world as the decisive focus for the spiritual vitality of others? Theologians who realize this problem seek to ameliorate the effects of this approach by pushing the problem to *the end of life*, i.e. after death there will be a post-mortem encounter with Christ for other believers. However, apart from the problem of giving encounter in post-mortem existence *per se* any clear sense, this does nothing to answer the central problem. The encounter with Christ as necessity is retained; only the manner and moment of encounter is postponed. The dilemma for Dialogue, even on this modified view, is illustrated neatly in a Vatican document from the late 1990s, which put the question: 'How can one enter into interreligious dialogue, respecting all religions and not considering them in advance as imperfect and inferior, if we recognise in Jesus Christ and only in him the unique and universal Saviour of mankind?'[16] This challenge remains unanswered in both official ecclesiastical theology and also much academic theology.

Approach (3) interprets Mission more in terms of the idea of 'human witness' than 'divine givenness': there is a narrative to recount of what has been experienced and discovered to be transformative but it will be open to other witnesses. Mission becomes Dialogue. In the final analysis, all traditions are rafts (to use a Buddhist image), means to an end, and they conceptualize these means and ends according to the best conceptual matrices that are available. But all matrices are necessarily limited – they involve pointers, metaphors and symbolic representations – and this is because religious language depicts but does not reproduce the ultimate truth of our condition and the meaning of life. The infinity of ultimate reality is the deeper ineffable ground of the many phenomenal manifestations of religious insight and truth. An empirical justification for hypothesizing this is that the traditions show themselves to be comparable at the empirical level – producers of both good and bad in spiritual insight and practice. No one tradition has been greater than another in history. It is important to stress that, on this view, radical differences are retained, for the religions are historically specific in so many ways, but their mutual belongingness in transcendence is also affirmed.

Some have objected to this third Pluralist outlook in so far as it seems to arrive at a tidy conclusion too rapidly. Religions, they aver, have different aims, different expected outcomes: what a Hindu or a Sikh might mean by 'salvation' is not the same as that which a Christian proclaims, and so on. We cannot therefore assume that we are all united, even in the realms of ineffable ultimate reality. There are just differences: we can respect one another, we can encounter without assuming superiority, we might even perceive something in the other that enriches our own outlook and which has emerged more fully in another tradition than our own. But don't assume we all meet somewhere, even if that somewhere is mystical. This is the objection of those who fit under the Particularist rubric.

My own reaction to this criticism is that it misses the mark. The Pluralist view is an inductive view. That is, it proceeds on the understanding that Christian faith is based on experience that can be trusted, and that there is no reason why this mechanism of trusting experience cannot be extended to others also. If this simple point is accepted then there is the challenge to make sense of the manyness of religious life as a matter of theological reasoning. Emphasizing the radical

> There is no reason why this mechanism of trusting experience cannot be extended to others also

differences between traditions reflects what is the case phenomenologically. But that does not prevent anyone making the inductive move that as Christian faith is not a projection but a trust of experience and a cognitive response to what we call the divine reality – and that this is partially confirmed by its spiritual fruits – so we can say the same is true for others. This leaves a problem: How to explain the diversity of religious life, assuming that the religious life is a valid life based on a varied sense of transcendence, and where the religions have displayed ethical and spiritual impressiveness and unimpressiveness throughout history in roughly equal measure? How to allow for radical differences and yet honour the assumptions, impact and discoveries of dialogue itself? Simply to say we are all different and that's that seems insufficient in the face of the evidence and the practice. Theology has to catch up with the practice.

Theology of religions *v.* Comparative Theology

In recent years, under pressure from so-called postmodernism, pressing the case for incommensurability between traditions has led some critics to conjecture that the whole attempt to construct any theology of religions is bound to be misconceived.

Even so, most are not content to let religions remain in their silos and are happy to promote dialogue, particularly dialogue around ethical issues or 'common good' politics and economics. The term most often used to aid this move is 'hospitality'.

Consider, for example, the following statements from the World Council of Churches document, 'Religious Plurality and Christian Self-Understanding': 'Our willingness to accept others in their "otherness" is the hallmark of true hospitality.'[17] And further: 'Our hospitality involves self-emptying, and in receiving others in unconditional love we participate in the pattern of God's redeeming love.' Certainly this bursts the bounds of exclusivity, but we can still ask the theological question: what does this mean for the acceptance of other traditions? The answer appears to move towards Pluralist thinking:

> We see the plurality of religious traditions as both the result of the manifold ways in which God has related to peoples and nations as well as a manifestation of the richness and diversity of human response to God's gracious gifts.[18]

'Hospitality' in this document – supported equally by the Commissions on Faith and Order, World Mission and Evangelism, and Interreligious Relations and Dialogue – is essentially an ethical category, intended to enhance the dialogue but without impugning Christian mission. Yet the transformation envisaged as a result of the dialogue is far-reaching:

> Hospitality requires Christians to accept others as created in the image of God, knowing that God may talk to us through others to teach and transform us, even as God may use us to transform others.
>
> The biblical narrative and experiences in the ecumenical ministry show that such mutual transformation is at the heart of authentic Christian witness. Openness to the 'other' can change the 'other,' even as it can change us. It may give others

new perspectives on Christianity and on the gospel; it may also enable them to understand their own faith from new perspectives. Such openness, and the transformation that comes from it, can in turn enrich our lives in surprising ways.[19]

'Hospitality' harbours theological expectations: through dialogue perspectives will be changed. The document does not advocate any particular theology of religions but it seems to me that theology of religions options cannot be left out of the picture.

The WCC document comes close to advocating what has become known in recent years as 'Comparative Theology'. This is not the comparison of religious beliefs and practices as in the old 'Comparative Religion' sense, but presents itself as an alternative theology to theology of religions. Feeling that the options of Exclusivism, Inclusivism and Pluralism are too abstract, too removed from taking account of how the religions actually are in history and reality, comparativists remain advocates of dialogue but shun theology of religions. Their interest is in the religions as more than simply cultural phenomena, but as they present experiences and ideas and witness to truth. This is theological engagement and it is recommended that Christians (and others) remain rooted in their own traditions as they pursue their comparative work. So James Fredericks advises Christians to live with the 'tension between commitment to Christianity and openness to other religious truth'.[20] This seems fine, for all of us are located somewhere irrespective of our tradition. But does that 'commitment' entail the finality of truth as a position which is non-negotiable? If so, then how does that square with assumptions about dialogue and about mutual learning; what would openness really amount to? Sooner or later questions of theology of religions cannot be avoided. This point has been well made by the theologian of religions, Perry Schmidt-Leukel:

The comparative theologian may start her work without any elaborated general theory of religion or without any explicit option of a theology of religions . . . However, the systematic and consequent pursuit of the comparison – if it is carried out theologically, that is with a prior interest in the truth and value of the investigated religious ideas or beliefs – will sooner or later lead to a point where the question of the relationship between the non-Christian and respective Christian beliefs becomes unavoidable.[21]

Comparative theology is not an alternative to theology of religions after all!

A similar point to Schmidt-Leukel's has also been made by the Catholic theologian, Paul Knitter. Analysing the proposals in the provocative and well-received book *The Im-Possibility of Interreligious Dialogue* by Catherine Cornille,[22] Knitter notes how the virtues proposed by the author resonate most satisfyingly with a Pluralist perspective. Cornille presents what is essentially an ethics for engagement/dialogue and incorporates five personal virtues as prerequisites for productive comparison. These are humility, commitment, trust in interconnectedness, empathy and hospitality. Cornille seeks to balance the preservation of identity – yes, even with its commitment to the fullness of truth residing in one's own revelation or tradition – with genuine and real openness to learning from others. Knitter notes how this tension is unsustainable and in effect requires a Pluralist theology of religions to resolve it. In Knitter's view, Cornille has a Pluralist model lurking within her explanations of the virtues. For example on 'hospitality' Knitter finds:

that in the way Cornille describes the practice of this virtue of hospitality, she ends up with a theology that is profoundly compatible with, if not identical to, what has been called the pluralist model. We must disarm ourselves of claims of fullness and finality and be ready to be surprised by truth that comes from the Other.[23]

73

Comparative Theology leans in the direction of Pluralism after all!

My thesis throughout this chapter has been that both Mission and Dialogue have had their suspicions of one another but the overtures that the one makes to the other require grounding in a theology of religions that enables the relationship to flourish. On the one hand, Mission must surrender the corner of the mind that assumes that one religion alone is eventually superior in terms of experience, insight and ethics. In which case we might agree with Cantwell Smith:

> Both Mission and Dialogue have had their suspicions of one another but the overtures that the one makes to the other require grounding in a theology of religions

> The future of the Christian mission turns on our learning to see God's mission in the Church as one part of his whole mission to mankind; not as his whole mission to one part of mankind (fallacy of indifference); nor as his sole mission to all mankind (the fallacy of arrogance).[24]

On the other hand, Dialogue must renounce the notion that all religions are variations on the same theme. In which case we might agree with Stanley Samartha:

> If the great religious traditions of humanity are indeed different responses to the Mystery of God or *Sat* or the Transcendent or Ultimate Reality, then the *distinctiveness* of each response, in this instance the Christian, should be stated in such a way that a mutually critical and enriching *relationship* between different responses becomes naturally possible.[25]

Mission supplies religious identity on which Dialogue thrives, and Dialogue becomes the new context within which Mission learns to practise the mutuality of authentic witnesses. Pluralism in the theology of religions arbitrates between the two.

5

Next steps

Over the past fifty years, theology of religions has moved towards centre stage for Christian thought. That is to say, it is no longer an 'afterthought' in manuals of Christian teaching. Does Christian faith see itself as God's only offer of salvation (transcendent vision and human transformation) for the world, or the best offer, or as one offer among others? This book has argued that new information from the lived experience of other believers moves us towards embracing the last of those three options. If this is correct, then we have reached a new moment in the unfolding of Christian history. The fact that the discussion about the place of 'other religions' in a Christian understanding of God's purposes is currently a raging discussion suggests that the new moment is not fully, or even in part, accepted. Abraham Heschel's remark with which this book began – 'In this aeon diversity is the will of God' – has still some way to go before it is convincing to responsible Christian theologians. But I have not found any alternative assessment of our religious situation among those who pull back from it.

It is sometimes claimed that Christianity has only recently become properly global, by finally escaping its European straitjacket. This might be true. But the globe is ineradicably plural. How Christian thought responds will determine its next phase in this century and beyond. Perhaps Christian thought will one day be written as a story of expanding consciousness – changing and being changed by interaction with different configurations of what human life has meant to many peoples.

This book has considered how Christian faith might interpret the ineradicably plural world of which we are a part. In this respect, it has been an exercise in expanding Christian consciousness. But the journey of expansion continues. Therefore I would like to put forward the following 'Paradigm' as a further framework within which Christians (and others) might interpret their place in a larger whole. First presented for public discussion in 2005 when it was published in the journal *Interreligious Insight* (I was one of its three author-editors), it strikes me still as a fitting possibility for 'the next steps' in the discussion of how to make sense of our current global plurality. As the 'Paradigm' picks up on a number of themes which have occupied this book, I offer it here as an invitation to enter more fully into the religious pluralism of our time.

The *Interreligious Insight* Paradigm[1]

As editors of *Interreligious Insight*, we believe that the experience of dialogue and engagement across worlds of religious difference represents a threshold phenomenon in our time. While the resources of our varied religious and humane traditions are available to help us negotiate this unfolding historical moment, there is a real sense in which we have

> Fresh models of what living positively with religious difference entails are being required of us

not been at this threshold before. Fresh models of what living positively with religious difference entails are being required of us.

It is no exaggeration to say that a powerful momentum is capable of being harnessed, as new opportunities for shared thinking and hopeful action across barriers of ignorance, suspicion and enmity are being explored.

We analyse this new phenomenon in terms of the following three dimensions:

1 as part of an expanding vision of global cultural evolution;
2 as an experience of religious pluralism that generates a dialogical understanding of religious truth;
3 as a profound ethical challenge to many of our inherited
   patterns of behaviour and attitude towards unknown others.

1 Sea change: cultural evolution in the twenty-first century

What would it be like to live in an age of astonishingly con-
tradictory values, an age on which a major value shift had indeed
descended? What would it be like to dwell in a time characterized
almost equally – on the one hand – by the declining influence
of time-honoured, long-dominant notions, assumptions and
predispositions, and – on the other hand – by the slow but
steady rise of countervailing ideas, hopeful models and new
inclinations? What would it feel like to stand in the very moment
of the value crossing? Would one be riding the old wave down
and out or the new one up and in? The questions are striking
and important because ours *is* in fact a period of dramatically
accelerated cultural evolution, an extremely rare period of 'sea
change'. It has two fundamental features:

- the seemingly sudden and precipitous decline of a long-
  dominant set of cultural values, ways of thinking, moral and
  ethical assumptions, and behaviours;
- the rise of a more complex, more *evolved* and more appropriate set of values, modes of understanding, moral-ethical
  insights, conscious choices, and ways of acting.

Table 1 (overleaf) offers a brief glimpse of some characteristic
values of the older and newer waves.

   The transition from the older to the newer complex of
values can be represented by the crossing of two waves. As the
long-dominant culture wave begins to decline in influence, the

Table 1 Transitions in values in the early twenty-first century

Older wave	*Newer wave*
Patriarchy	Gender equity, partnership
Inevitability and usefulness of war	Non-violent conflict resolution, 'soft power'
Inevitability of social imbalance and injustice, universal human rights as unattainable	Social and economic justice and human rights as realizable goals
Manipulation of the environment for humans	Ecological sensitivity and sustainability
Cultural superiority, triumphalism	Intercultural respect and mutuality
Northern domination of the Global South, colonialism	Global North–South cooperation
Disparate and divisive views of world problems and solutions	Emerging global consensus on approaches to peace, justice and eco-sustainability
State power	Emerging influence of non-state actors, global civil society
Unilateralism on the international stage	Multilateralism in global affairs
Religious exclusivism	Religious inclusivism and pluralism, global interreligious movement
Declining interest in spirituality	Deepening of spiritual practice
Mind and body as separate entities	Exploration of the mind–body connection
Higher learning dominated by isolated disciplines	Interdisciplinary, *integral* approaches to learning and knowledge

energy of the new wave grows. The decline and advance result directly from the increasingly poor fit of old wave values with new realities and new understandings. Transition is triggered by the build-up of *anomalies*, which are observed realities that contradict assumed 'facts'. In a given cultural period, when the build-up of anomalies reaches a critical level, certainties begin to erode. Once in a very great while, when the dissonance is intense enough, things that are known 'absolutely' are no longer certain at all and a sea change is under way.

The most important feature of the two-wave model is the period of crossing itself. There must come a point when the influence of the declining older wave and that of the ascending newer wave are approximately equal. That passage will necessarily be marked by chaotic change, vanishing certainties, identity crisis and extremism. It will also be enriched by new understanding, energy, commitment and spiritual growth. We believe that it has now arrived.

But there is a pressing question. If ours is indeed a time of rapid cultural change for the better, why does everything so often seem so wrong? Part of the answer is to be found in a phenomenon we might call an 'eddy'. When the rhythm of a smoothly flowing stream is disturbed, eddies can form. These are usually temporary whirlpools, roiling the water in their immediate vicinity but not significantly affecting the prevailing flow. In a time of major evolutionary culture change, when prevailing patterns are being disrupted, a disturbance is created in the life experience of individuals or groups. If either a sufficient number of persons or groups are affected or significant concentrations of power are challenged, a major counter flow can form, and this is an 'eddy'. The analogy is apt. In the context of the two-wave model, an eddy is a discernible and often destructive pattern of *resistance* to the decline of the older wave and the advance of the new.

One can identify any number of distinct eddies, including:

- identity politics
- religious and political fundamentalism
- religious or nationalist extremism and terrorism
- increasing violence against women

- anti-ecological intransigence
- neo-imperialism
- suspicion of scientific understanding.

But in every case, there exists persuasive evidence that the pattern in question does not represent the 'cutting edge' of cultural change. It is, rather, a reaction against the value change that is the real transformation. A reaction such as fundamentalism may create enormous (and dangerous) turbulence in a changing world; it is extremely unlikely, however, to reverse a powerful evolutionary flow. Some of the critical problems of our age need to be understood not as aspects of the declining older wave – and certainly not as features of the newer wave – but as *phenomena of the crossing.* They are dangerous but temporary counter flows that can slow but not stem the new tide.

The *Interreligious Insight* Paradigm draws on the two-wave ('sea change') model as a powerful tool for analysing and addressing most of the polarizations that are so characteristic of the early twenty-first century – everything from global violence to globalization, from relations among nations to relations among religions, from evolution to genetics, from gender roles to gay rights, and from liberal-conservative politics to justice and peace. Understanding the dynamics of cultural evolution frames the new polarizations and suggests tools for understanding, engaging, and even healing the rifts.

> One central component of cultural sea change is interreligious dialogue

One central component of cultural sea change is interreligious dialogue. The following section explores this dimension further.

2 Interreligious dialogue: a way to truth

Dialogue means 'speaking across' worlds of difference. It is to be differentiated from both old-style monologue and redundant-style relativism. Monologue assumes that there can only be one authentic religious vision and relativism assumes that we simply have to live with a confusion of competing voices. Being able to 'speak across' worlds of difference both overcomes the isolation of monologue and refuses the fate of relativism. What remains is the conversation.

We used to perceive the religious Other as an object of suspicion or threat. In dialogue, however, the religious Other is no longer a de-humanized object but a living subject from and with whom we can learn. Potential enemies are converted into potential partners. Religious vision and the possibilities for making a difference in the world are enriched because they are shared. As a consequence, the potential for religiously motivated violence recedes.

Dialogue is both a process and a new way of articulating the varied transcendent vision and human transformation that lies at the heart of the religious approach to life. As a process, dialogue depends on giving and receiving: we offer the wisdom, values and truth of 'my' tradition and we open ourselves to other articulations of the same. The process assumes at least the following attitudes and values:

- listening for authenticity
- respect for differences
- willingness to learn from the other
- self-criticism
- moving beyond absolutism
- leaving behind relativism
- forging criteria to distinguish between true and false religious belief and practice.

The dialogical combination of commitment with openness creates a dynamic momentum in which identity is forged afresh. Corners of the mind which retain superiority are surrendered in a process that is never-ending.

As a new way of pursuing religious truth, dialogue accepts that *relationship* between traditions assumes paramount importance: we define truth as both-and and not as either-or. In this mode, we are likely to welcome complementarities of vision over against the competition of visions associated with absolutism and relativism. We give full rein to the recognition that no one tradition can comprehend the fullness of ultimate truth. The distinction between the hidden mystery of ultimate reality and the apprehension of that reality in historical forms is key to fruitful dialogical encounter. All traditions embody some version of this distinction. Its corollary is that human language is necessarily indirect when it comes to describing our experience of ultimate reality.

In dialogue, partners articulate their basic experiences and developed traditions in conversation with one another. They will learn about each other and in particular be challenged to overcome stereotypical images of one another. Such images are deep-rooted and demand hard listening on the part of participants, but the fruit will be new discoveries. As trust grows, participants learn tolerance of one another, yet they may still keep a respectful distance. We exist alongside one another in parallel lives and the negotiation of similarities and differences begins in earnest. Eventually, dialogue leads to a deeper interaction whereby participants move beyond tolerance and learn to live within the space between different basic visions. This is a space that is vulnerable and risky, but its fruit is the mutuality of belonging: we become a community of communities.

The space between the assumption that 'we're all the same' and the insistence that 'we're all different' is where dialogue flourishes. Plainly, the religions are not all the same – we have different origins, histories and spiritualities. Yet neither are they all different, in the sense that no family resemblances can be discerned between them. We inhabit one earth and we have powers to exercise human empathy across many boundaries. Followers from many traditions seek transcendent vision and human transformation, *no matter how variously these are shaped symbolically and worked out in practice.* If we were all the same there would be no need to talk to one another; if we were hopelessly sealed in separate rooms there would be no possibility of talking at all!

The giving and receiving of dialogue is hard spiritual work. For this reason, dialogue aims to embody relationships of trustful acceptance, critical friendship and mutual accountability. We are neither quick to judge nor uncritical in outlook. Worlds of difference really are strange to one another. Yet the ability to 'speak across' worlds of difference means that we are able to resonate with the authenticity of the subjective other. We are many communities yet one community; we are far apart yet belong together. In dialogue, we move between strangeness and resonance.

Dialogue does not take place in a decontextualized bubble. Traditions encounter one another on a global canvas. Religious truth is a transforming truth and therefore it exists for the sake of making a difference in the world. In this sense, a dialogical community of interreligious being and activity becomes a model community in the transformation of all life. Justice, peace, sustainability, compassion and community are articulated and lived out as a collective witness to the global future. The world needs religions in conversation, not religions in competition.

Let us say that interreligious dialogue is both what the world yearns for from the religions and what the religions at their best do offer. It is more than a process and represents a paradigm shift in religious consciousness. As such, it becomes a central component in the sea change of global evolution.

3 Interreligious engagement: a moral code of practice

Modern means of transport and communications have annihilated distances and brought peoples of the world nearer to one another than ever before. No country, culture or religious tradition remains any longer in isolation. Every part of the world is increasingly becoming multireligious and multicultural. Although the world has become small, it remains culturally and religiously very rich.

> Every part of the world is increasingly becoming multireligious and multicultural

In the emerging global environment, we welcome these diverse currents of world religions and their potential contributions to the welfare of humankind and the planet as a whole. The religions are vehicles that enable humanity's search for those deeper truths and realities that motivate us and point us towards a fulfilling vision for the future.

At the beginning of the twenty-first century, the world faces a whole range of conflicts which can be analysed in multiple forms – religious, socio-political, economic, environmental and existential. Given that the roots of conflict are often complex it is generally more helpful to see the various analyses as inter-related. In turn, this means not only that destructive individual behaviour needs changing but also that destructive institutional behaviour needs to be confronted.

At their best, the religions point to a basic spiritual requirement of transcendent vision and human transformation at the heart of all human endeavour, individual and collective. This requirement may be channelled differently by the religions, but all believe that basic moral and human values stem from it. The 'golden rule' in one form or another and the exhortation to transcend the ego are present in all religions. All teach that human relationships are more important than our material possessions. All teach that service of the poor, the sick, the helpless and the oppressed is service to that which transcends all of us, however it is named. It follows that the different religions should cooperate with one another in dealing with basic personal and institutional structural problems.

If the religions are to influence humankind for good and work for the development of all peoples, then they must put their own houses in order first. They have too much to lose by staying apart, and so much to gain by working together. They must learn ways both of healing the legacy of history's bitter interreligious rivalries and of celebrating the positive experiences of cooperation from the past. When religions meet one another, they must learn to combine trust with critical fellowship.

The time is ripe for a reorientation of the religious outlook on a world scale. We have to relinquish inherited prejudices so that we can live with open hearts and minds. In the interests of forging peaceful interreligious relations, we offer a Code of Practice which includes at least the following recommendations:

1 Respect the noble teachings and values of others' religions.
2 Acknowledge the rights of others to follow their own paths.
3 Respect the civil and political rights of religious minorities.
4 Promote constructive steps towards interreligious harmony.
5 Take positive steps to heal the religious antagonisms of the past.
6 Refrain from abusing others' religious beliefs and practices.
7 While commending one's own religion, avoid condemning one's neighbour's.
8 Forbid violence against innocent persons, men, women or children, in the name of religion.
9 Prevent gender, racial and ethnic discrimination in the name of religion.
10 Relinquish religious biases and prejudices, inherited or acquired.
11 Work together for the sake of establishing spiritual and humane values at the heart of life.

12 Be open to the best influences that stem from modern knowledge and serious investigation of both the natural world by the sciences and the human world by the humanities and social sciences.
13 Adopt a critical attitude towards your own perspectives before criticizing others.

Not all religious beliefs and values are compatible with one another. But it is likely that many perspectives will be complementary to one another. Where we differ profoundly we shall need to learn respect. Where a religion promotes violence or oppression in violation of the Code of Practice it is to be condemned. Not everything labelled spiritual or moral is acceptable.

The world has suffered too much because of wars fought in the name of religion. There has been enough of finding fault in and condemnation of others' religions in history. The attitude of intolerance has not brought and cannot bring peace and happiness to any society or nation or to humanity at large. The exaltation of terrorism in the name of religion is particularly tragic. The third millennium requires a spirit of mutual respect and cooperation among the followers of different faiths.

The great religions are not the possession of one community or group; they belong to humanity. They should firmly and cooperatively raise their voices, individually and collectively, against the menace of violence and war, terrorism and extremism, and against social, economic and racial injustices. This entails challenging the institutions that shape our world in the public square with the basic spiritual and moral values that we all share.

Furthermore, the religions should emphasize that the means adopted to solve these problems should be in keeping with the dignity of humanity. Religious leaders must make a commitment to talk together, walk together and work together for the welfare of humanity.

Religious pluralism is a fact; the great religions are forces to be reckoned with. Vast resources and power for good resides in them. But they are frequently misused and exploited for selfish and narrow purposes. Individual and collective egos overemphasize the parochial and ignite religious rivalries. Through self-criticism and dialogue there lies another way.

This '*Interreligious Insight* Paradigm: An Invitation' is offered as a new means for understanding the religious complexity that is emerging in our times. It believes that we do stand on the threshold of a different way of being religious. Moreover, it is hopeful in so far as it seeks a new vision. There are signs of positive change in the direction that we have sketched. But the scope for further change is endless.

Appendix
A letter to Gandhi from Charles F. Andrews[1]

Your talk on religion yesterday distressed me, for its formula 'all religions are equal' did not seem to correspond with history or with my own life and experience. Also your declaration that a man should always remain in the faith in which he was born appeared to be a static conception not in accordance with such a dynamic subject as religion.

Let me take the example of Cardinal Newman. Should he, because he was born in Protestant England, remain a Protestant? Or again, ought I, in my later life, to have remained a rigid Anglo-Catholic, such as I was when I came out to India? You, again, have challenged Hinduism and said, 'I cannot remain a Hindu, if untouchability is a part of it.' I honour you for that true statement.

Of course, if conversion meant a denial of any living truth in one's own religion, then we must have nothing to do with it. But I have never taken it in that sense, but rather as the discovery of a new and glorious truth, which one had never seen before and for which one should sacrifice one's whole life. It does mean also, very often, the passing from one fellowship to another; and this should never be done lightly, or in haste; but if the new fellowship embodies the glorious truth in such a way as to make it more living and real and cogent than the old worn-out truth, then I should say to the individual, 'Go forward; become a member of the new faith which will make your own life more fruitful.'

But let me repeat with all emphasis, this does not imply the denial of any religious truth in what went before. It does not mean for instance that a Christian is bound to believe that only Christians can be saved. My dearest friend, Susil Kumar Rudra, declared openly that he cherished all that was good in Hinduism and yet he was a profound Christian.

This attitude of Susil's (which has now become my own) is surely in accord with the mind of Jesus Christ. We find that Christ welcomed faith (i.e. trust in God's power to save) wherever He found it . . . When the pagan Roman centurion came to Him, 'I have not found,' He said with great joy, 'such faith, no, not in Israel.' To the Greek Syro-Phoenician woman, He said, 'O lady, great is thy faith.' Not only are abundant examples given of this manner of life which He pursued, but the essence of all His teaching was that God is our Father and that there are no favourites among His children . . .

It is well also to notice His utter condemnation of those who seek at all costs to gain converts to their own religion . . .

To repeat, Christ is to me the unique way whereby I have come to God and found God and I cannot help telling others about it, wherever I can do so without any compulsion or undue influence. The Khan Sahib equally holds that Islam is the unique way to God, and I would most gladly sit at his feet, as you and I have both done, in order to find out more and more what Islam means to him; and I would sit at your feet also to find out what Hinduism means to you . . .

As far, then, as I can read His life, Christ deliberately broke down every barrier of race and sect and reached out to a universal basis. He regarded His message as embracing the whole human race.

I find that Buddhism is a universal religion of a similar world-wide character. It went out from India all over the world and I honour it for doing so. Personally I am thankful that the Ramakrishna Mission is doing the same today and I have had true fellowship with its missionaries in America, Australia and Europe.

Also I find historically that Islam was proclaimed a universal religion; and I have lived in the families of devout Muslims in different parts of the world with great happiness and shared many of their ideals.

Thus I find that universal note, beyond the boundaries of a single city, is common to these living religions of mankind. Perhaps you would be surprised if I called you the greatest exponent of Hinduism today in the whole world. If a living truth is held with all the soul, as you hold it, you cannot help proclaiming it . . .

But you may answer, 'That means we shall always be fighting as to whose "Gospel" is superior; and this will bring with it all the evils of "compassing sea and land to make one proselyte."'

I don't think that follows. Let us look at it this way. I feel, as a devout Christian, that the message which Christ came into the world to proclaim is the most complete and most inspiring that was ever given to man. That is why I am a Christian. As you know well, I owe everything to Christ.

But I must readily concede to my dear friend, the Khan Sahib, Abdul Ghaffar Khan, whom I love with all my heart for his goodness, exactly the same right to hold that the message of the Prophet Mohammad is to him the most complete and most inspiring that was ever given to mankind. That is why he is a Mussalman. Since it is to him a living truth, I fully expect him to make it known. He cannot and should not keep it to himself.

And you surely have the abundant right to proclaim to all the world the living truth of Hinduism which you regard as the supreme religion (Parama dharma).

I do not think that the act of Christian Baptism militates against the idea which I have propounded in this letter, or implies the renunciation of anything that is good in Hindu or Islamic culture. The exact phrase is that we renounce 'the world, the flesh and the devil,' that is to say, the essential evils of this life. I know that this would imply for a Christian the renunciation of certain things in Hinduism which you would think unobjectionable, such as idolatry, but there are Brahmos who renounce idolatry and yet remain Hindus. I do not want to be vague myself here and I feel that there are clear-cut distinctions between Christians, Hindus and Muslims, which cannot be overpassed. But I do not think that we need to anathematise one another in consequence. We should rather seek always to see the best in one another; for that is an essential feature of love.

There is a precious element of goodness which we can all hold in common . . .

That seems to me a fine way towards peace in religion, without any compromise, syncretism, or toning down of vital distinctions.

I have written this in as objective as possible, when dealing with a subject so charged with emotion as religion is to me. I look forward to the time when the noble phrase of the Qur'an Sharif, 'Let there be no compulsion in religion,' will be true all over India and throughout the world. It is the great ideal at which all of us should aim . . .

Notes

Introduction

1 Abraham Joshua Heschel, 'No Religion Is an Island', in Harold Kasimow and Byron L. Sherwin (eds), *No Religion Is an Island: Abraham Joshua Heschel and Interreligious Dialogue* (Maryknoll, NY: Orbis Books, 1991), p. 14.

2 Heschel, 'No Religion Is an Island', p. 13.

3 Heschel, 'No Religion Is an Island', p. 16.

4 Stanley Samartha, the Indian Christian theologian and first Director of the World Council of Churches' Sub-unit on Dialogue, formed in 1968, once asked the question echoing Heschel: 'Can it be that it is the will of God that many religions should continue in the world?', in *One Christ – Many Religions: Toward a Revised Christology* (Maryknoll, NY: Orbis Press, 1991), p. 79.

5 According to A. F. C. Wallace there have been at least 100,000 religions on Planet Earth since the evolutionary emergence of human beings. See A. F. C. Wallace, *Religion: An Anthropological View* (New York: Random House, 1966), p. 3.

6 Yann Martel, *Life of Pi* (Edinburgh: Canongate Books, 2003), p. 48.

7 Martel, *Life of Pi*, p. 49.

8 Readers could consult any works by Raimon Panikkar, Klaus Klostermeier or Bede Griffiths.

9 Martel, *Life of Pi*, p. 57.

10 Martel, *Life of Pi*, p. 58.

11 Martel, *Life of Pi*, p. 61.

12 Martel, *Life of Pi*, p. 61.

13 Martel, *Life of Pi*, p. 62.

14 Jalaluddin Rumi, 'The One True Light', in *Rumi: Poet and Mystic*, trans. R. A. Nicholson (London and Boston, MA: Unwin Mandala Books, 1978), p. 166.

15 Martel, *Life of Pi*, p. 69.

1 Using Scripture in theology of religions

1 Oscar Cullman, *From East and West: Rethinking Christian Mission* (St Louis, MO: Chalice Press, 2004), p. 121. Cited in Kenneth Cracknell, *In Good and Generous Faith: Christian Responses to Religious Pluralism* (Peterborough: Epworth Press, 2005), p. 3.

2 Donald Senior and Carroll Stuhlmueller, *The Biblical Foundations for Mission* (London: SCM Press, 1983), pp. 339–40.

3 Cracknell, *In Good and Generous Faith*, p. 38.

4 Senior and Stuhlmueller, *The Biblical Foundations for Mission*, p. 345.

5 Cracknell, *In Good and Generous Faith*, p. 32.

6 See Heikki Räisänen, *Marcion, Muhammad and the Mahatma: Exegetical Perspectives on the Encounter of Cultures and Faiths* (London: SCM Press, 1997).

7 Räisänen, *Marcion, Muhammad and the Mahatma*, p. 15.

8 Wilfred Cantwell Smith, 'Idolatry', in John Hick and Paul F. Knitter (eds), *The Myth of Christian Uniqueness: Toward a Pluralistic Theology of Religions* (Maryknoll, NY: Orbis Press, 1987), p. 54. This whole essay is worthy of careful reading on this subject.

9 Cantwell Smith, 'Idolatry', p. 61.

10 Cracknell, *In Good and Generous Faith*, p. 59.

11 Senior and Stuhlmueller, *The Biblical Foundations for Mission*, p. 345.

12 See my own chapter, 'The Jewish-Christian Filter', in *Interfaith Encounter: the Twin Tracks of Theology and Dialogue* (London: SCM Press, 2001), for further reflections.

2 Between Exclusivist-Repudiation and Inclusivist-Toleration

1 Alan Race, *Christians and Religious Pluralism* (London: SCM Press, 1983).

2 The essay by Perry Schmidt-Leukel, 'Exclusivism, Inclusivism, Pluralism: the Tripolar Typology – Clarified and Reaffirmed', in Paul F. Knitter (ed.), *The Myth of Religious Superiority: A Multifaith Exploration* (Maryknoll, NY: Orbis Press, 2005), pp. 13–27, sets out many of

the objections to the typology and also answers them robustly
and deftly. See also essays in Alan Race and Paul M. Hedges,
Christian Approaches to Other Faiths (London: SCM Press, 2008).

3 Cited in Daniel Strange, 'Perilous Exchange, Precious Good News:
A Reformed "Subversive Fulfilment" Interpretation of Other
Religions', in Gavin D'Costa, Paul Knitter, Daniel Strange, *Only
One Way?* (London: SCM Press, 2011), p. 129.

4 Emil Brunner, *Our Faith* (London: SCM Press, 1936), p. 16.

5 Strange, 'Perilous Exchange, Precious Good News', p. 99.

6 Strange, 'Perilous Exchange, Precious Good News', p. 101.

7 Emil Brunner, *Revelation and Reason* (London: SCM Press, 1947),
p. 270.

8 Cited in Richard J. Plantinga (ed.), *Christianity and Plurality: Classic
and Contemporary Readings* (Oxford: Blackwell, 2007), p. 248.

9 Plantinga, *Christianity and Plurality*, p. 257.

10 Justin, *Apologia*, I.xlvi.2–3, in André Wartelle (ed.), *Saint Justin:
Apologies* (Paris: Etudes Augustiniennes), 160.1–10, 1987, and cited
in Alistair McGrath, *The Christian Theology Reader* (Oxford:
Blackwell, 1995), p. 320.

11 *Nostra Aetate*, in Austin Flannery OP (ed.), *Vatican Council II, The
Conciliar and Post-Conciliar Documents* (Dublin: Dominican
Publications, St Saviour's, 1975), p. 739.

12 *Nostra Aetate*, p. 739.

13 <www.vatican.va/roman_curia/congregations/cfaith/documents/
rc_con_cfaith_doc_20000806_dominus-iesus_en.html>.

14 Karl Rahner, *Foundations of Christianity* (New York: Crossroad,
1982), p. 139.

15 See the Anglican report, *The Mystery of Salvation: The Story
of God's Gift*, a Report by the Doctrine Commission of the General
Synod of the Church of England, Chapter 7, 'Christ and the world
faiths' (Trowbridge: The Cromwell Press, 1995); also, Amos Yong,
Beyond the Impasse: Toward a Pneumatological Theology of Religions
(Grand Rapids, MI: Baker Academic, 2003); David Cheetham,
'Inclusivisms: Honouring Faithfulness and Openness', in Race and
Hedges (eds), *Christian Approaches to Other Faiths*, Chapter 4.

3 Between Pluralist-Acceptance and Particularist-Refusal

1 The phrase is from Langdon Gilkey, 'Plurality and Its Theological Implications', in John Hick and Paul F. Knitter (eds), *The Myth of Christian Uniqueness: Toward a Pluralistic Theology of Religions* (Maryknoll, NY: Orbis Books, 1987), p. 37.

2 Ernst Troeltsch, *The Absoluteness of Christianity and the History of Religions* (London: SCM Press, 1972), p. 126. The citation is from Clement of Alexandria.

3 Daniel O'Connor, *Gospel, Raj and Swaraj: The Missionary Years of C. F. Andrews 1904–14* (New York: Peter Lang, 1990), p. 11.

4 O'Connor, *Gospel, Raj and Swaraj*, p. 260.

5 John Hick, 'The Next Step Beyond Dialogue', in Paul F. Knitter (ed.), *The Myth of Religious Superiority: a Multifaith Exploration* (Maryknoll, NY: Orbis Books, 2005), p. 12.

6 See Perry Schmidt-Leukel, *Transformation and Integration: How Inter-faith Encounter Changes Christianity* (London: SCM Press, 2009).

7 Rosemary Radford Ruether, 'Feminism and Jewish-Christian Dialogue: Particularism and Universalism in the Search for Religious Truth', in Hick and Knitter (eds), *The Myth of Christian Uniqueness*, pp. 137–42.

8 Ruether, 'Feminism and Jewish-Christian Dialogue', pp. 137–42.

9 See Paul Hedges, *Controversies in Interreligious Dialogue and the Theology of Religions* (London: SCM Press, 2010), pp. 146–96, for a comprehensive account of 'Particularities' and critique.

10 Joseph A. DiNoia, *The Diversity of Religions: a Christian Perspective* (Washington, DC: The Catholic University of America Press, 1992), p. 63.

11 James L. Fredericks, 'A Universal Religious Experience? Comparative Theology as an Alternative to a Theology of Religions', *Horizons* 22 (1995), pp. 83–4.

12 Keith Ward, 'Pluralism Revisited', in Sharada Sugirtharajah (ed.), *Religious Pluralism and the Modern World: An Ongoing Engagement with John Hick* (Basingstoke: Palgrave Macmillan, 2012), p. 63.

13 Cited in David J. Bosch, *Transforming Mission: Paradigm Shifts in Theology of Mission* (Maryknoll, NY: Orbis Books, 1991), p. 489.

14 George Lindbeck, *The Nature of Doctrine: the Church in a Postmodern Age* (London: SPCK; Philadelphia, PA: Westminster Press, 1984).

15 Lindbeck, *The Nature of Doctrine*, p. 42.

16 Gavin D'Costa, 'Christianity and the World Religions: A Theological Appraisal', in Gavin D'Costa, Paul Knitter, Daniel Strange, *Only One Way?* (London: SCM Press, 2011), p. 22.

17 See, for example, Gavin D'Costa, *Theology and Religious Pluralism* (Oxford: Blackwell, 1986).

18 Paul Hedges, *Controversies in Interreligious Dialogue and the Theology of Religions* (London: SCM Press, 2010); Perry Schmidt-Leukel, 'Religious Pluralism and the Need for an Interreligious Theology', in Sugirtharajah (ed.), *Religious Pluralism and the Modern World*, pp. 19–33.

19 H. M. Kuitert, *Jesus: The Legacy of Christianity* (London: SCM Press, 1998), p. 129.

20 See, for example, Bede Griffiths, *The Marriage of East and West* (London: Collins Fount, 1983).

21 See Rose Drew's compelling book, *Buddhist and Christian? An Exploration of Dual Belonging* (London: Routledge, 2011).

22 Marianne Moyaert, 'Postliberalism, Religious Diversity, and Interreligious Dialogue: A Critical Analysis of George Lindbeck's Fiduciary Interests', in *Journal of Ecumenical Studies* 47.1 (Winter 2012), pp. 64–86.

23 Cited in Moyaert, 'Postliberalism, Religious Diversity, and Interreligious Dialogue', pp. 73–4.

4 Between Christian mission and interfaith dialogue

1 'The Two Parliaments, the 1893 Original and the Centennial of 1993: a Historian's View', in Wayne Teasdale and George F. Cairns, *The Community of Religions: Voices and Images of the Parliament of the World's Religions* (New York: Continuum, 1993), p. 25.

2 See Marcus Braybrooke, *Pilgrimage of Hope: One Hundred Years of Global Interfaith Dialogue* (London: SCM Press, 1992).

3 Swami Vivekananda, <hinduism.about.com/od/vivekananda/a/vivekananda_speeches.htm>. Accessed December 2012.

4 Swami Vivekananda, <hinduism.about.com/od/vivekananda/a/vivekananda_speeches_2.htm>. Accessed December 2012.

5 Cited in Wesley Ariarajah, *Hindus and Christians: a Century of Protestant Ecumenical Thought* (Grand Rapids, MI: Eerdmans, 1991), p. 25.

6 For a full and excellent discussion of the Edinburgh conference and related theological discussion, see Kenneth Cracknell, *Justice, Courtesy and Love: Theologians and Missionaries Encountering World Religions, 1846–1914* (London: Epworth Press, 1995).

7 'The Baar Statement', *Current Dialogue* 19 (WCC, 1991), <www.oikoumene.org/en/resources/documents/wcc-programmes/inter-religious-dialogue-and-cooperation/christian-identity-in-pluralistic-societies/baar-statement-theological-perspectives-on-plurality.html>. Accessed December 2012.

8 'Humankind from the Age of Monologue to the Age of Global Dialogue', in *Journal of Ecumenical Studies* 47.3 (Summer 2012), p. 470.

9 Irving Greenberg, 'Judaism and Christianity: Their Respective Roles in the Strategy of Redemption', in Eugene J. Fisher (ed.), *Visions of the Other: Jewish and Christian Theologians Assess the Dialogue* (New York: Paulist Press, 1994), p. 24.

10 From Paul Mojzes's '28 Guidelines for More Successful Dialogue' in his essay, 'The What and the How of Dialogue', in Darroll Bryant and Frank Flinn (eds), *Inter-Religious Dialogue: Voices from a New Frontier* (New York: Paragon House, 1989).

11 *Redemptoris Missio*, Encyclical of John Paul II, 1990, in David R. Brockman and Ruben L. F. Habito (eds), *The Gospel Among the Religions: Christian Ministry, Theology, and Spirituality in a Multifaith World* (Maryknoll, NY: Orbis Books, 2010), pp. 137–9.

12 *Redemptoris Missio*, pp. 137–9.

13 Congregation for the Doctrine of the Faith, *Dominus Iesus: on the Unicity and Salvific Universality of Jesus Christ and the Church*, par. 22. Posted at <www.vatican.va/roman_curia/congregations/cfaith/documents/rc_con_cfaith_doc_20000806_dominus-iesus_en.html>. Accessed December 2012.

14 On the occasion of the publication of his book, *Why We Should Call Ourselves Christians: The Religious Roots of Free Societies* (2008; English language edition – New York: Encounter Books, 2011). Pera was formerly president of the Italian Senate and also a professor of philosophy at the University of Pisa. See the report by the *National Catholic Reporter*, 24 November 2008, at <bit.ly/TisNKE>. Accessed December 2012.

15 Hendrik Kraemer, *The Christian Message in a Non-Christian World* (London: Edinburgh House Press, 1938), pp. 216–17.

16 International Theological Commission, *Christianity and the World Religions* (Vatican City: Libreria Editrice Vaticana, 1997), p. 15.

17 WCC, 'Religious Plurality and Christian Self-Understanding', *Current Dialogue* 45 (July 2005), <wcc-coe.org/wcc/what/interreligious/cd45-02.html>. Accessed December 2012.

18 WCC, 'Religious Plurality and Christian Self-Understanding'.

19 WCC, 'Religious Plurality and Christian Self-Understanding'.

20 James L. Fredericks, *Faith Among Faiths: Christian Theology and Non-Christian Religions* (New York: Paulist Press, 1999), p. 170.

21 Perry Schmidt-Leukel, *Transformation and Integration: How Inter-faith Encounter Changes Christianity* (London: SCM Press, 2009), p. 99.

22 Catherine Cornille, *The Im-Possibility of Interreligious Dialogue* (New York: Crossroad Publishing, 2008).

23 Paul F. Knitter, 'Virtuous Comparativists are Practicing Pluralists', in Sharada Sugirtharajah (ed.), *Religious Pluralism and the Modern World: An Ongoing Engagement with John Hick* (Basingstoke: Palgrave Macmillan, 2012), p. 53.

24 Wilfred Cantwell Smith, 'Mission, Dialogue, and God's Will for the World', in *International Review of Mission, Tambaram Revisited* 78.307 (July 1988), p. 367.

25 Stanley Samartha, *One Christ – Many Religions: Toward a Revised Christology* (Maryknoll, NY: Orbis Press, 1991), p. 86.

5 Next steps

1 Reproduced here in slightly different form, this statement was initially authored by Alan Race, Jim Kenney and Seshagiri Rao and

published in the journal *Interreligious Insight* 3.1 (January 2005); it can be accessed at <www.interreligiousinsight.org/January2005/Jan2005.html>. If readers have any responses that they would like to make then the editors would be pleased to receive them. Send to <information@interreligiousinsight.org>.

Appendix: a letter to Gandhi from Charles F. Andrews

1 *The Guardian*, 4 March 1948, pp. 99–100. Daniel O'Connor (introd.), *The Testimony of C. F. Andrews*, published for The Christian Institute for the Study of Religion and Society, Bangalore (Madras: CLS, 1974), pp. 118–22.